RE:INVENT
YOUR LIFE!

WHAT ARE YOU WAITING FOR?

RE:INVENT
YOUR LIFE!

WHAT ARE YOU WAITING FOR?

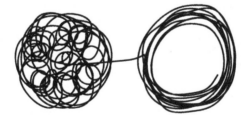

KATHI SHARPE-ROSS

FOREWORD BY
QUINCY JONES

*RE:*INVENT YOUR LIFE! WHAT ARE YOU WAITING FOR?

For information about this title or to order other books and/or electronic media, contact the publisher:

The Reinvention Exchange/THE SHARPE ALLIANCE, INC
www.TheReinventionExchange.com
Kathi@TheReinventionExchange.com

ISBNs:
978-1-7333930-0-3 (print)
978-1-7333930-1-0 (eBook)

Printed in the United States of America

Editor, Writer, Guide, Friend . . . beyond: Brooke White — brookewhite.info
Cover and Interior design: Marc Friedland & Melissa Bierlein — Couture Communications

re·in·ven·tion

rēin'ven(t)SH'n/

noun

the action or process through which something is changed so much that it appears to be entirely new

TABLE OF CONTENTS

PART 1: REALIZATION

PART 2: THE WORK

PART 3: EXCUSES, EXCUSES

PART 4: REALITY CHECK

PART 5: INSPIRATION

ACKNOWLEDGMENTS

It Takes a Village . . . always has, always will . . .

Bobby – my high school sweetheart and husband of 31 years, who supported me by being an amazing and involved father to our boys. He is my rock who has enabled me to always fly

My boys – Brandon and Jake, who are my everything at all times — my heartbeat, my life, my pride, my joy, my loves

Brooke – my brilliant editor, my friend, my inspiration, my sounding board, my co-spirited writer, my loving taskmaster

Carolynn – my best friend, sister, spirit guide, ground zero, mentor, inspiration, playmate and most stylish person I know

Chopin and **Al Green** – the soundtrack to my writing, lifted my soul . . . the perfect writing formula

Marc – my brilliant branding and creative genius, who so generously created the fabulous cover, brand direction and inspiration when I needed it most

Tami – who found me Brooke, and makes me laugh — author, friend and advisor

Auntie Natalie – who inspired me to know that we can have it all, gracefully, forever my home base

Marla – my lifelong truth, soul sister, bestie and fellow musketeer

Marci – my North Star inspiration, cheerleader, force of life, playmate always

Tobi – my book "muse," amazing friend, life coach and fellow musketeer forever

Stacey – my newest BFF, motivator, foodie partner . . . when it matters most

Jessica – my original editor who took years of "stuff" and made sense out of it

Autumn – sage friend, writer, executive, holder of truth and found me Jessica

My parents – who made me who I am . . . at least in the beginning 😊 — love you

And all my friends who have lovingly waited patiently and curiously for my book and inspired me every step of the way!

I have great gratitude for everyone that was interviewed for this book— for being courageous enough to share your story, willing to open up and expose the inspiration, the bumps in the road, the truth about the challenges you went through and the amazing outcomes you have created with your life. It is by sharing your journey with others that they will be encouraged and inspired to pursue their own dreams. I thank you for your time and I applaud you for being the amazing friends that you are. Keep Reinventing!

Thank you for allowing me to live this inspired journey!
Always be Reinventing — it's your lifeblood! #HappyReinventing

A special thank you to my wonderful friends and colleagues who shared their *RE:*INVENTION stories for this book.

In Order of Appearance:

Bob Wosnitzer	Daryn Kagan	Marla Baldassare
Cal Fussman	Lesley Jane	Jenifer Kramer
George Leon	Seymour	James Orsini
Scott Neitlich	Gaye Dean	Amy Lorbati
James Damian	Shannon Babcock	Lori Geller
Lisa Licht	Brad Jakeman	Marci Freedman
Maureen Barten	Linda Sivertsen	Lori Sale
Matt Hanover	Chris Pepe	Robin Cousins
Beth Comstock	Valerie Lewis	Ilene Sykes
Shelley Zalis	Stephanie Sperber	
Charlie Engle	Diana Nyad	

I also wanted to acknowledge the following individuals whose influential work was referenced throughout the book.

Dr. Aaron Beck	Dr. Gail Mathews
Arianna Huffington	Dr. Patrick Porter
Richard Hytner Consigliere	Gary Vaynerchuck
Chase Jarvis	

FOREWORD

When I was working on *Thriller*, the press kept talking about how I was a "sell-out" and that I had betrayed my jazz roots; well, my response to that was, you better know how to sell out and have something to sell. Often times, I find that society tries to put you in a box because the individuals in it are all stuck in one together, but I think that the ones who make it out are the people who remain in constant pursuit of maximizing their potential. Kathi is undoubtedly amongst the few who have made it out, and not only did she escape, but she is helping others do the same.

I first met Kathi when she was consulting on the "We Are the Future" humanitarian concert I put on in Rome back in 2004 at Circus Maximus, and we continued to work together throughout the years on many different occasions. Our latest collaboration included my "Quincy Jones Curated Collection" of ThinOptics reading glasses, where we partnered with ArtLifting artists to help provide opportunities for the differently abled communities. Through this partnership, we were honored to have raised money for Keep Memory Alive, ArtLifting, and the causes that my Quincy Jones Foundation supports. Kathi is always thinking outside of the box and that's why she continues to make something out of nothing.

I've had innumerable setbacks in my life, but each time, I used those moments as fuel for my next endeavors, because I knew that if I simply dwelled on the negativity, I would have been pulled further back each time. I believe that we are the biggest barriers to our own creativity and growth because of paralysis from analysis. When I was learning how to score films, one thing I learned from my mentors (Victor Young at Paramount and Alfred Newman at Fox) was to never look back. They'd tell me, just write and turn the page! Even if it doesn't make sense to you in the moment, write it down! You are your own biggest writer's block and it's time you stop monitoring yourself and let. It. FLOW!! In the same way, you've got to stop monitoring your every move, and live. Your. LIFE!!

Kathi, big-time love and props to you for not only figuring IT out for yourself, but for sharing IT with the rest of us in this book and your everyday life. You only live once, so keep on keepin' on!!

— QUINCY JONES

PREFACE:
MAKE YOUR OWN LUCK

Some of us are born lucky. I'm not referring to beauty, money or power. I'm talking about purpose. Fulfillment. Happiness. Some of us are born with a natural inclination to follow our hearts and put our dreams in motion.

Others find their purpose through Reinvention — the action or process through which something is changed so much that it appears entirely new.

I was one of the lucky ones. My parents always told me I could do anything I set my mind to. And I believed them. By the time I was 14, I'd already lived in three countries: Australia, Israel and the United States. I'd been exposed to cultures, languages and opportunities most kids my age never imagined. I'd lived with privilege and culture and was exposed to the horrors of war and death before I even learned who The Beatles were at the age of twelve! I inherited my father's "itchy feet" and my mother's deep inner strength, spirit and wisdom. I had the self-confidence to travel the world and conquer it — all before I finished high school. How I ended up so "well-adjusted" is anyone's guess.

Growing up in Australia, I was in awe of my Auntie Natalie. I spent most weekends at her house so I could play with my cousins. She was a PR executive in the film business, and she was the quintessential working mother.

One of my favorite places to explore was her home office — the smell of papers, her typewriters, the books on the shelves. It had a sense of busy, organized chaos and something special being created.

My aunt eventually became one of the most successful and recognized business leaders in Australia. Subliminally, I must have considered her my first role model. I just didn't know it till years later, when I realized what my "norm" was and how naturally it came to me, all as a result of seeing her do it back then. She was juggling a business, a family and an amazing and conscientious husband.

When I was growing up, my parents gave me a sense of confidence and a "can-do" attitude. There was never a "box." We stepped out of our comfort zone by traveling and frequently uprooting ourselves as a family. The world didn't seem big and scary to me, because I got to experience it with my own eyes at a young age.

Unlike a lot of people I know, I have never suffered from life confusion. My Ah-Ha Moment came early. I thought I would love marketing and public relations. I knew I wanted to work for myself, as I have a free spirit and love people and their stories. I just followed that instinct.

By my senior year of college, I was running a successful shirt design and jewelry business — one that started on my living-room floor. I turned my talent for knowing what people wanted to buy into a full-fledged money-making business. When I graduated from college, I wasn't looking for a job. I already had one.

I saw a big, wide future in front of me and was in no hurry to go work in a conventional office under someone's thumb. While my friends interviewed for jobs in their skirt suits and pearls, I took the entrepreneur's path and sold Kathi's Kostume Jewelry to retail stores. I grew the business nationally through local manufacturers and sales reps. All the sorority girls and Madonna fans in my college town of Santa Barbara were adorned in my colored Swarovski rhinestones and baubles. It seemed so straightforward: I made the jewelry, people loved it, I sold it, I made money.

Out of college, and after a few years, the mental stimulation just wasn't there anymore. I still wanted to keep my fun jewelry business as a side hustle but needed to buckle down and start doing something that felt more like a career instead of a hobby.

I had a pretty good sense of the path I would take and some great role models to emulate. The summer before I graduated, I interned for my older sister at her PR company, where I was exposed to some amazing women business owners. They all shared an office suite and ran their own companies.

When the time came to move in a new direction, I tapped into my contacts and went to work with one of the PR execs. Soon after, my sister moved overseas to expand her business, and I jumped in to help her run her PR company. She left me holding the reins on a lot of responsibility, which I easily absorbed and eagerly took on. Creating business, running the accounts, and being in charge felt comfortable.

Managing the company was the perfect launch pad. I was able to focus on brands and campaigns that were interesting to me on a personal level, and I had the chance to challenge myself by creating additional services. We quickly changed the business dynamic into two separate companies, and I now owned SHARPE PR & MARKETING and surrounded myself with a great staff that brought new skills and expertise to grow the business from a PR company into a full-scale Marketing, PR, Promotions and Sponsorship Agency. We did business with colleagues in LA, New York, Sydney, Paris and Hong Kong.

Every day, and at every opportunity, I grew the business and the scope of our services. The notion of building clients' brands and initiatives, helping define who they were and contributing to their successes was enthralling.

My passion for marketing grew, and I grew along with it. My education took place in the "classroom of LIFE." I read, listened to, and learned anything and everything about many industries, disciplines and ideas. I couldn't get enough and had such a thirst for knowledge and growing. I found everything so interesting and wanted to be a part of so many worlds. Being my own boss gave me the freedom to truly explore life on my terms.

I didn't realize until much later what a free spirit I was, because all I ever seemed to do was work. As they say, "If you love what you do, you'll never work a day in your life." I don't know if that's exactly true in my case, as I've been going 24/7 for about 30 years — with the last 15 years running the newly renamed THE SHARPE ALLIANCE — and my work is a core part of who I am and how I choose to live. My life's work has been a constant Reinvention.

Satisfaction in my career led to happiness in other aspects of my life. It allowed me to build the family I dreamed of and find the right life partner who understood me and allowed me to fly.

People always say to me, "Oh, Kathi, you're so lucky." Well, yes, I was lucky to be born to parents who instilled a sense of adventure and possibility in me, but the rest of it was by design and came through intentional hard work and following what I knew I naturally loved. Luck had very little to do with it.

At every stage of my life, I've envisioned what I wanted the outcome to be and created a plan to get there. *I gave myself permission to listen to that little voice inside me that told me to push harder, to switch gears, to double back, to slow down, to hurry up, to pause, to celebrate, to love. And now I want to share that concept with you.*

This is *not* a self-help book. I'm not a life coach or a therapist. There is no hard science behind my approach. I'm a marketing guru. A businesswoman. A mother. A wife. A daughter. A friend. In my line of business and in my personal life, I see countless men and women, every day, living lives that leave them Restless. Unhappy. Exhausted. Lonely. Longing for something more.

This book is about making your life just what you want it to be. It's about taking the first step from an Ah-Ha Moment and transforming it into your *personal* Ah-Ha Movement! It's about recognizing your dream and putting it in motion — perhaps for the very first time. It's about SAVING YOUR LIFE — because you have only one. It's about what's possible and giving you the tools to explore it yourself — because you can!

> *"Tell me — what is it you plan to do with your one wild*
> *and precious life?"*
> — Mary Oliver, *"The Summer Day"*

At its heart, this is a Reinvention Roadmap, to set you on the path for a life of greater happiness and deeper fulfilment with a richer sense of purpose. The book is full of real stories about real people who realized they wanted — needed — to Reinvent their lives. It's about Reinventing the whole self — careers, marriages, interests — and most importantly, mindset. It's about self-worth and self-wonder. It's full of tips, ideas — and even lessons learned — to help start your own Reinvention.

Reinventions come in all shapes and sizes — whether it's a five-minute adjustment or a ten-year plan, it all counts, and it's important for you to know the value of a Reinvention, no matter how big or small.

Indeed, it doesn't matter how old you are, how much money you make, or where you are in this journey. It is a process, and I can certainly attest to that. When I set out to write this book and start TheReinventionExchange.com, I had to figure out how it would fit into my family and business schedule. The biggest challenge was how to prioritize my already-precious time.

I decided even if it took me 10 years to write a book — and it has — I'd stay the course. I bit off small pieces along the way, wrote a blog for the *Huffington Post* for nine years and then started writing for *Thrive Global.* I constantly posted pieces of inspiration on social media, did speaking engagements and was interviewed on podcasts. I sent newsletters out to my business community and friends, who encouraged me with their interest in the subject, their excitement and their feedback and stories they wanted to share. Slowly, I chipped away at the process of writing this book, because I wanted to inspire and impact others. Plus, the feedback re-inspired me, time and time again.

The theme of this book hasn't changed throughout these years, but the world, our life pace and the content have all evolved from when I first began, frankly, making it more topical now than ever before. So, stick to your dream if you really want it — the clock belongs to you, and you are free to do with it as you wish! It's always the right time to Reinvent the life you want.

INTRODUCTION: NOW WHAT?

I was sitting in the audience of my oldest son's high school graduation when it hit me: this was it.

This was the moment, at our graduation — the very last moment I can remember when all of my friends agreed on one simple fact: the world was ours to conquer. We were free. We were hell-bent on changing everyone and everything. We had a great sense of adventure and were ready to leave the nest and fly. We knew we could do it. No doubts. No stress. No worry. Just excitement and anticipation for all that lay ahead of us.

Then what?

Fast-forward 20 years, and many of my friends — men and women alike — were singing a different tune. Most had done well on their chosen career paths. They had money. They had families. Nice cars and homes. They were "successful" by any typical definition. But that twinkle — that spark within many of them — was gone.

The trend was so widespread in my personal and professional circles that I set about trying to understand it. Why were so many smart, healthy, successful people so unhappy? Why were so many of my friends out of tune with life?

As the owner of a successful brand and marketing agency, I help people Reinvent their companies, their brands and in many cases, their personal goals and visions for their lives all the time. Markets change. Consumers move in different directions. Technology evolves. Companies need to Reinvent themselves if they want to thrive. They have to maintain a competitive edge by being informed and constantly evolving.

The cycle of business got me thinking: maybe, as humans, we need to Reinvent our lives as well. Reinvention enables us to thrive and maximize our journey on this Earth. When we truly understand Reinvention, we allow ourselves to constantly grow and evolve. I'm not talking about branding or self-promotion. I'm talking about looking at ourselves honestly and asking, "Could my life be better than it is at this moment? Could I be happier, more fulfilled, have more fun, reach my dreams, and live up to my greatest potential? Right here, right now?" And if the answer is "Yes," we need to rethink our strategy. We need to be willing to Reinvent our lives.

"UM . . . HOW DID I GET HERE?"

I hear this question a lot from friends and colleagues, whether we're sitting in a meeting in their corner office or grabbing drinks in any spot around the world. How did I get to this place, where my job runs my life? When did my spouse become like a stranger to me? How do I no longer have time for running, yoga, guitar — (you name it) — and yet, I devote countless hours to strangers, to devices, to a career that doesn't inspire me anymore?

On the surface, the answer seems simple. As we get older, our priorities shift. We commit to our jobs and careers. We focus on taking care of our partners, children and loved ones. We stop *doing the things that make us happy* and default to merely *doing* (bills, work, carpool). We think that growing up means letting go — letting go of our dreams and focusing on our increasing responsibilities rather than on our own happiness.

We ask, "How did I get here?" with a tinge of shame. It feels like a dirty secret to admit we're unhappy, so we accept the stress, anxiety and depression as unavoidable consequences of adulthood. We turn to bad habits — drinking, overeating, cheating and overspending to make ourselves feel better. *We'd rather waste our lives than admit we want to change them.*

For me, the question, "How did I get here?" is one of the most exciting, inspiring questions I can imagine someone asking me. It means someone is finally ready. Ready to take the first step in rediscovering that excitement — fulfillment — joy — they felt on the day of their high school graduation. It means they're ready for Reinvention!

PART 1: REALIZATION

CHAPTER 1

WHAT IS *RE:*INVENTION?

"Every day, you reinvent yourself. You're always in motion.
But you decide every day: forward or backward."

— James Altucher

Reinvention is a personal intervention with yourself. Reinventions come in all shapes and sizes. But at the heart, it requires taking an honest look at what you want and what you love. What real steps can you take right now to make those things a bigger part of your life?

What does that first leap of faith look like? Is it starting that diet you've been putting off, or telling your boss you want a raise, or leaving your job to open that little chocolate store in the middle of Main Street? Maybe you are ready to move on from a bad relationship, or start some charity work, or go horseback riding, or meditate every morning for five minutes.

Sometimes Reinventions are big. Starting a new career. Rebuilding a relationship with a family member or friend. Addressing a substance-abuse problem. Rediscovering your faith. Reconnecting with your partner. Other times, they're subtler. Revisiting a childhood love of music.

Playing a bigger role in your spiritual community. Making time for a date night with your partner.

Regardless of its size, Reinventions have one thing in common. *Like an intervention, Reinventions can change your life — even save your life — if you let them.*

I know what you're thinking.

"I'm busy. I don't have time to change my life right now! I'll think about it during vacation next summer." Or maybe you never will.

There is no single more important task in your life right now than being happy. Period. Being happy and feeling fulfilled will make you a better partner, a better parent and a better provider than you ever imagined. Nurturing your happiness should be the very first item on your to-do list every day.

YOUR HAPPINESS QUOTIENT

So what does happiness mean to you? If happiness is the catalyst for your Reinvention, you need to understand how you define it and where it fits into your life. This will be your *why* for every step of your Reinvention journey. It will be your holy grail, your goal, your end game and possibly your ever-shifting finish line as you explore more and more ways to Reinvent your life.

Some define happiness by their successes in business; some define it by the love in their lives. Others find it in their family, a healthy lifestyle, their faith or their friendships. Waking up each day with a sense of joy, purpose and inspiration can be enough to make you happy.

We all have different interpretations at different stages in our lives. Only you can decide what your happiness quotient and score-card look like. So, if Reinventing any piece of your life is going to make you happier in any way, shape or form, allow yourself to get clear on *why* you need to make some changes, and then you can figure out *how*.

You may be shy, scared, insecure or uninspired. There could be a million reasons why you're not yet ready to tackle this important question and shake things up in your life. But imagine: isn't it worth giving your spirit the sense of freedom that comes with making impactful decisions and changes? Freedom unlocks greater control and confidence. It reinforces the fact that you *can* have what you want in your life and you *can* be happy. That freedom is your right, your entitlement and your gift.

"The secret of happiness is freedom, and the secret of freedom is courage."
— Thucydides *(471 BC–400 BC)*

Today, it may be the decision to learn a language, pick up a guitar or play tennis every week. Tomorrow, who knows what you might want to explore on a larger scale: career options, new relationships, favorite hobbies, childhood dreams? The options are endless.

What do you need in (or out of) your life to be who you want to be and have all that makes you happy?

"Freedom is the oxygen of the soul."
— Moshe Dayan

In the following pages, you'll find exercises — aka Power Tools — that will help you unearth your own Ah-Ha Moment — however small or large it may be. Don't freak out! This is the exploration phase. It's the time to let your heart rise to the surface and find out what "happy" really means. Are you ready to roll up your sleeves?

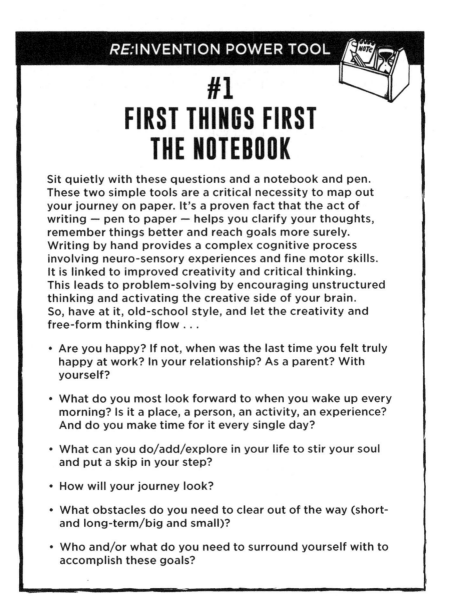

RE:INVENTION POWER TOOL

#1
FIRST THINGS FIRST
THE NOTEBOOK

Sit quietly with these questions and a notebook and pen. These two simple tools are a critical necessity to map out your journey on paper. It's a proven fact that the act of writing — pen to paper — helps you clarify your thoughts, remember things better and reach goals more surely. Writing by hand provides a complex cognitive process involving neuro-sensory experiences and fine motor skills. It is linked to improved creativity and critical thinking. This leads to problem-solving by encouraging unstructured thinking and activating the creative side of your brain. So, have at it, old-school style, and let the creativity and free-form thinking flow . . .

- Are you happy? If not, when was the last time you felt truly happy at work? In your relationship? As a parent? With yourself?

- What do you most look forward to when you wake up every morning? Is it a place, a person, an activity, an experience? And do you make time for it every single day?

- What can you do/add/explore in your life to stir your soul and put a skip in your step?

- How will your journey look?

- What obstacles do you need to clear out of the way (short- and long-term/big and small)?

- Who and/or what do you need to surround yourself with to accomplish these goals?

We have to be able to recognize the moments of happiness in our lives and celebrate them. For me, it's been singing to the radio, a nice long, hot shower, a walk down six flights of stairs, a trip to the manicurist, driving the kids to school and listening to their stories, game night with friends, a walk on the beach, outings to the museum and theatre, cooking a new recipe for the family and chocolate! The little things add up, so identify what those "happy moments" look like, and really appreciate their value in your life.

Do you allow yourself these small indulgences and, better yet, recognize them in your everyday life?

RE:INVENTION POWER TOOL

#2
MAKE SOME LISTS

- Make a list of 10 things that put a smile on your face or nurtured your soul in the last few weeks.

- Notice where they occurred, who you were with and why they made you feel good. You'd be surprised at how much you take for granted.

- Now, make a list of 10 things that you want to do in the next few weeks that will realistically fit into your life routine.

Give yourself something to smile about.

Your happiness is the destination, so go for it.

Maybe you already know exactly what you want, but you're not quite sure how to get started. Or maybe — like a lot of us — you can sense something is off. It's gnawing away at you. You know there's more to life than what you're living, but you're not quite sure what you need to do to make it better. You're not alone in this feeling. This is a big issue for a lot of people.

No matter where you are on the journey, *I want this book to take you to the next step. I want it to take you from dreaming to doing — no matter what your personal Reinvention might be.*

"

AND THE DAY CAME WHEN THE
RISK TO REMAIN TIGHT IN A BUD
WAS MORE PAINFUL THAN THE RISK
IT TOOK TO BLOSSOM.

— ANAIS NIN

As you'll see in these pages, everyone's story is different. There is no right or wrong way to be happy, and there is no good or bad time to reach for that happiness. Will it always end up perfectly? No. Life rarely does. But in taking risks and making bold choices, every lesson learned offers a richer life experience.

For some, that day comes in a flash. Life strikes them like lightning, and they know it's time to take a leap. For others, it's more of a quiet tug. A little voice that's been calling — for months or even years — begging them to burst out of the bud they've been wrapped up in so tightly. My only request is that you *listen to that voice. Follow it. Push beyond the excuses, and let it guide you to the life of your dreams.*

Throughout this book, I've included tools to help you, no matter what stage of the Reinvention journey you may be on. Skim it. Think on it. Set it down for a minute. Settle down with some coffee and a blanket. Use it to keep the sparks flying — or to get them going in the first place. After all, *your inner spark is nothing until you allow it to light up the world.*

> *"The universe buries strange jewels within us all and then stands back to see if we can find them."*
> — Elizabeth Gilbert, *Big Magic*

Each of us was born with giant, gleaming, gorgeous jewels within us. Maybe a little jagged, maybe in need of polishing. But still, for many of us, these gems are (as yet) undiscovered. We favor security (or our own *in*securities) over the gifts we were born to explore or achieve.

Reinvention is about returning to the days of discovery. It's about pulling out your tools — your shovel, your hammer, your pick ax or

"

YOU GET TO CREATE YOUR LIFE — NOT JUST SIT BACK AND BE.

your chisel — and finding that sparkly, shiny, invaluable center that is perfectly you.

Not all tools work for everyone. Some people like to hack away at the hard parts. Others like to gently brush the surface until the dust clears. Whatever your method, please know: It is never too late. It is never too soon. It is always the perfect time to connect with a happier, more fulfilled, more joyous you.

CHAPTER 2

THE AH-HA MOMENT

"Most of us have two lives. The life we live,
and the unlived life within us."
— Steven Pressfield

The most important part of any Reinvention is the very first step: Realization. Awaken to that voice within that says you need a change. Many of us have spent months — years, even — sublimating that voice. We've made excuses. Told ourselves we're too old, too poor, not good enough, not smart enough, not worthy enough or not entitled to expect more from our lives.

The Realization phase of your Reinvention is about taking out the earplugs, drowning out the background noise and listening — truly listening — to your whole, authentic self.

Part of that listening is actively assessing all aspects of your earthly world to find your pain points and understand where you could benefit from a change. The process will be different for all of us.

"

WE ALL HAVE THE ABILITY TO HAVE
AN AH-HA MOMENT. THE THING
THAT SEPARATES US IS WHETHER
WE HAVE THE COURAGE TO FOLLOW
WHERE THOSE MOMENTS LEAD.

I look at my friend, Bob Wosnitzer, who was making six figures trading on Wall Street, when he realized he needed a change. After years of drug and alcohol abuse (so common in his business), and a bit of a wake-up call, he decided to clean up his act and get sober. Couple that with a bad breakup, and Bob knew he needed a new perspective. His was an Ah-Ha *Movement* in the making.

We've all had these moments! Maybe not all at once, like Bob, but suddenly, it hits us: the career we've spent years (or possibly even decades) building just isn't for us. We feel it. We know it. But somehow, we don't scream, "I got it!" in the way we could.

THE ART OF LISTENING

A lot of us ignore those moments. We tuck them away in the back of our mind, choosing to think of them only in the dark, when no one is looking, when no one can judge us or tell us we're crazy for wanting to do something different with our lives, whether it is going back to school, joining the church choir, or revisiting a long-lost love of photography. I've seen it hundreds of times, and if you ask me, it's time to start listening to yourself. This comes down to the difference between those who do and those who don't!

Bob left his high-powered career to go back to school for an entirely different field, media studies. One of his goals when he embarked on his return to school was to let go of any preconceived "results" and remain open to the possibilities that came his way. He recognized that learning a new subject could lead to anything, be it a career in film production, teaching — or even the realization that media studies wasn't his calling after all.

Ah-Ha Moments are everywhere. But do you hear them, and are you aware of the true impact they can have on your life?

Reinventing your life is all about the Ah-Ha Moments. The moment when you acknowledge that, no matter where you are, there's something else you want to do, feel, live or engage in, and you recognize it. If you listen carefully to yourself, you'll notice clues that will lead you to what you wish you were doing, creating, living and being.

When you meet someone who's doing what they love with their life, ask them what their Ah-Ha Moment was. Their response may help you look for the clues about where to find your own. Some had it at a young age, and others didn't have it until after they turned 50.

They are your moments, and they're so quietly yours that you may not even realize how powerful they really are. Don't take that inner voice for granted next time you have an Ah-Ha Moment: listen, take note and start the process of your life Reinvention.

While an Ah-Ha Moment can come quite suddenly for some, do not fear if it takes more time for your Realization to hit you. Just as it has taken years to build into your current life situation, it can take some time to spiral out of it. The process of doing your own work and uncovering your own truths is the first — and most important — step in the Realization process, no matter how long it takes.

Indeed, one thing I have learned from interviewing countless souls who have pursued their own Reinventions is that the journey — this journey you are now beginning — is an important and cherished part of the experience. The process of self-discovery, or re-discovery, is invaluable and should never be rushed or overlooked.

"An open mind will open your life."
— Anonymous

FLASH FORWARD

Cal Fussman's early journalism career is a true testament to the power of listening for your own Ah-Ha Moment. Periodically throughout his life, he's been presented with clear and defining moments of choice, all led by his insatiable curiosity and interest in challenging himself to live outside his comfort zone at every turn. Each time an opportunity came up, it was the same — a moment of reflection that naturally inspired him to go for the unknown and the discovery, practically creating his own Ah-Ha Moments over and over. He would be going about his business, functioning in a happy place, and then a fork in the road appeared. He could either stay put or chase the unknown. Each time, he had to follow his instinct to find the best course forward.

He shared the story of the first time this happened to him over lunch not too long ago. At 22, Cal got a job he thought he would have for the rest of his life. As a kid, he wanted to be a sports columnist for a daily paper. Those guys ruled their towns. Everyone read them, respected them, and talked about their work. So, Cal went to journalism school at the University of Missouri. After graduation, he landed a plum position at *The Miami Herald*. He was on his way to realizing that childhood dream.

A year later, *The St. Louis Post-Dispatch* called and wanted to talk to him about writing for the sports section. This was what he'd always wanted. The only catch was he'd have to come in as the number-2 guy. Everyone else on staff was between the ages of 35 and 60. They'd all been through the school of hard knocks, and the editor didn't want to cause a mutiny by bringing in a 23-year-old rookie. He'd have to pay his dues, too. After a year, Cal started to get noticed around town. Despite his number-2 position, there was still resentment toward him from the veterans at the paper.

One Saturday night, he submitted a story about a baseball game. When it ran the next morning, someone (he never found out who, but he has an idea) had replaced a quote from the pitcher with an inaccurate statement. He'd been toyed with, putting Cal's reputation and credibility with the players on the line. It was a sucker punch that caused him to snap to.

Suddenly, he saw the next 40 years flash in front of his eyes. Was this the kind of crap he was going to have to put up with? Petty games and backstabbing from other jealous reporters?

He faced a hard choice. Stay in St. Louis, a place he loved with every fiber of his being, where everything was laid out for him, or take a stand, shuffle the deck, change his destiny, and bounce into the unknown.

He chose the latter. He walked into his managing editor's office the next morning and announced he was moving to New York. He'd already secured a position at a new sports magazine he'd done some freelancing for.

This was Cal's Ah-Ha Moment! Some might view his decision as an extreme moment of self-awareness and bravery. Cal's father didn't see it that way. He saw it as reckless and irresponsible, but Cal had to listen to that inner voice that told him, "This is not the life for me. I have to move on, and the time is now." I applaud him for listening to his gut and taking a hard right outside of his comfort zone.

Cal's early Ah-Ha Moment changed the trajectory of his entire career. He's one of the most beloved and respected writers in the business today. He's even got a new career twist (aka Reinvention!) — a podcast series, "Big Questions," where he interviews some of the most intriguing personalities from all walks of life. Cal's curiosity has driven his passion for life and all that he does.

THE DOORS

Sometimes, Ah-Ha Moments are symbolic. For me, doors symbolize a gateway to something different. These possibilities all stand just on the other side of that symbolic door — so close, and yet so far away.

"When one door closes, another door opens, but we so often look so long and so regretfully upon the closed door that we do not see the ones which open for us."

— Alexander Graham Bell

Doors separate rooms, attitudes, experiences and activities. They have their own distinct space, but an open door brings them together, blending the energy of two different rooms. As you step through the door, the new environment is usually in deep contrast to the other, retaining traces of the old but promising the experience of a fresh start.

The metaphor of a door captures the moment in time when we're on the threshold of a movement, a decision or an opportunity. Everything we want seems to stand on the other side of that door. Today, let's try to unlock it.

We stand in the familiar with a vision of what's on the other side. We can choose to walk through the door or stand in the frame until we're ready for something new. Or we can stand exactly where we are, looking at the door, and longing for what's on the other side.

These defining moments, whether small or large, are the doorways of your life. They offer either opportunity or confinement. *The choice is always yours. When the doorways to Reinvention are in front of me, I usually run through them, excited to approach what's next.*

What does a door represent for you? Pull out that notebook and think about those doors you have closed, those you are standing in front of and those that you've walked through. Give great thought to the relevance of those moments when you were at a critical juncture in your life and the impact of those moments.

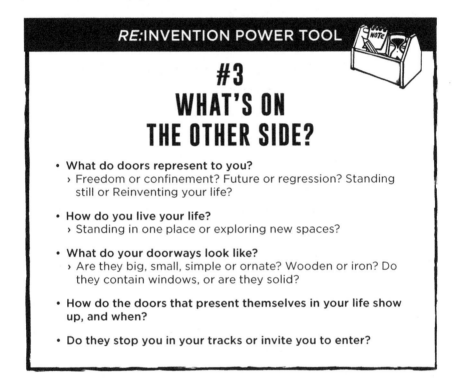

RE:INVENTION POWER TOOL

#3
WHAT'S ON
THE OTHER SIDE?

- **What do doors represent to you?**
  › Freedom or confinement? Future or regression? Standing still or Reinventing your life?

- **How do you live your life?**
  › Standing in one place or exploring new spaces?

- **What do your doorways look like?**
  › Are they big, small, simple or ornate? Wooden or iron? Do they contain windows, or are they solid?

- **How do the doors that present themselves in your life show up, and when?**

- **Do they stop you in your tracks or invite you to enter?**

As you dig in to unearth the answers to these questions, A Word to the Wise: be open to what you may find. Do your best to let go of old expectations and ideas of success, worth and happiness. *You must be open minded for new doors to reveal themselves — or just go open them yourself, and see what lies before you!*

*RE:*INVENTION INTROSPECTION

My friend George Leon spent years in denial about what his true calling and purpose in life was, and it kept him in a corporate job much longer than he should have been. His overpowering ego anchored him in a constant struggle with who he was, what he wanted to do and where he wanted to go. After quitting his extremely demanding entertainment-studio job, George "publicly took a year off" but was quietly anxious about what his future held and continuously turned down consulting jobs, finding they didn't align with his perception of what he thought his strengths were.

This deep soul-searching period was so important to his Reinvention. He truly believed he was more intelligent, qualified and skilled for these positions. George was in denial about what he was actually good at, instead focusing only on what he *thought* he was good at. Feeling confused and lost, George was afraid that his ego would prevent him from ever finding work again. He looked at himself as a fraud, fearing that his charm was the only reason for his success. George had to start re-evaluating his strengths.

Sometimes great things happen in "moments of grey." Surprisingly, George arrived at his Ah-Ha Moment during a presentation for a consulting company, which he was reluctantly working on at the suggestion of a colleague. He truly shined, and it was in this moment that he realized where his true talents lay, and the direction became clearer. George forced himself to go back to school and to sharpen his skills by enrolling in a social media course at UCLA. Not only did the class teach him valuable information, but, more importantly, it gave him the confidence to continue pushing forward and forge his new path with excitement.

For George, self-doubt was his biggest enemy. However, once he was able to finally trust and believe in himself and his true strengths, the self-loathing slowly started to fade away, and he found himself doing all that comes naturally to him and that he's good at.

Coming to the realization that you need to Reinvent does not always come easily. A lot of the time, we're constantly fighting with the demons inside our own head. When we can fully accept and understand our flaws and all, the final step toward Reinvention draws closer and closer.

George's true fear was of aging out of the industry, and this made him overcompensate and rely on skills that kept holding him back. He believed in himself for the wrong reasons. However, with the help of some good friends, a supportive partner, and valid self-realization, George was eventually able to find his true talents, and he is now the founder and creator of his own entertainment marketing agency. He certainly Reinvented his attitude, career and life in meaningful ways.

George now understands that, *"What you believe to be true may not be what others believe to be true about you."* We are all living and hoping for a happier and healthier life. However, we are the only ones who can help ourselves in finding this. George knows that this is just one of many Reinventions he is destined for in his lifetime!

CHAPTER 3

HELLO? ARE YOU STILL IN THERE?

"Don't you find it odd that when you're a kid, everyone, all the world, encourages you to follow your dreams. But when you're older, somehow they act offended if you even try."

— Ethan Hawke, *The Hottest State*

I agree with Ethan Hawke — somehow, somewhere, many of us have lost our natural instinct to follow our dreams. *Let this book be a compass to find your way back to yourself.*

When one of my sons was younger, people always asked him what he wanted to be when he grew up. His eyes would light up like sparklers when he heard the question, and he'd answer with all the confidence of a five-year-old: a Karate kid, a race-car driver, a policeman, a Power Ranger (all at the very same time). His enthusiastic response was followed by colorful stories of the places he'd race, the bad guys he'd catch, and the planets he'd conquer and save. And we never once told him he couldn't do it.

Later, he had grandiose ideas of products he'd invent. His imagination ran wild with possibility while he sat in the back of my car. Back then, his stories were full of joy, hope and confidence because those were the only things he knew. He hadn't yet encountered societal pressures. He didn't feel compelled to base his career on how much money he would make or on what others would think of him. He didn't even know what money was.

I miss those days. Not just for him, but for all of us. I miss when he couldn't wait to jump out of bed. The days I'd have to pry him away from his Hot Rod cars and LEGOs for meals and potty breaks; he was so lost in play and joy that he literally forgot he was hungry or tired or cold.

What made *you* leap out of bed or caused you to get lost for hours as a child? Do you remember?

If we think hard enough, most of us can probably name a dream we held onto back then that we never followed or dropped too quickly. Years passed, and we had to triage our responsibilities. And when that happens, dreams are easily buried under a pile of laundry, or bills, or work-related activities or you name it. Reality gets in the way, but now it's time to clear the decks and get some clarity.

The beauty of Reinvention is that sometimes, by revisiting our childhood dreams, we can find where we were really meant to be, before "real life," in all of its messy glory, got in the way.

"Dig deep in your soul to recover the person you once were before you became what someone else wanted."
— Anurag Prakash Ray

Our earliest inclinations in life are good indicators of our strengths and, ultimately, the kind of work that brings us joy. While you might think that flying to the moon, becoming a rock star, or playing professional hockey are a little unrealistic at this point in your life, that's OK.

Tailoring your dreams to fit your life right now — joining a garage band, signing up for the regional hockey league, or coaching a kid's team — can go a long way toward creating the joy you've been longing for.

RE:INVENTION POWER TOOL

#4
WHAT DO YOU WANT TO BE
WHEN YOU GROW UP?

Let's start here.

What were you doing when you were 5 years old, maybe 12, perhaps 17? What did you dream about doing? Did you want to be a rock star, an artist, a fireman, a dancer?

Close your eyes, and think of what you used to imagine your life would be like "one day." Give yourself permission to dream as you did when you were a child.

- What did you want to be when you "grew up"?

- What activities did you spend hours and hours doing?

- Where did your imagination take you?

- When did you drift away from those dreams, and why?

- Was it because you lacked the skill or the confidence to pursue them?

- Or did you simply lose interest in singing, dancing, flying to the moon, driving race cars, being an inventor?

- Have you tried picking these dreams up at any point in your life again?

- Where is the butcher, the baker, or the candlestick maker of your youth?

- When did you stop driving the train and become a passenger?

- *What* do you *want to be* 1, 5, 12, 17 years from today?

- *Where* do you want to be, and *why*?

Let's put everything that "real life" tells us to do aside for a spell and get back to our real selves. Peter Pan, the boy who never grew up, said, "Once you grow up, you can never come back." I disagree! You're never too old to access those dreams that drove you to make a microphone out of your hairbrush, build a ladder to the sky out of the pillows from your bed, or make a spaceship out of old boxes in the garage. *Imagination is a powerful tool. Dust it off!*

FEED YOUR SOUL

When we let our dreams go, we let part of ourselves go with them. We get grumpy. We get angry and resentful. We start to assume things will never work out for us. We have an empty spot in our hearts that never feels full, no matter what we do.

> *"The tragedy of life is in what dies inside a man while he lives."*
> — Norman Cousins

The little rock star grew up. He went to school, he got a job, he started a family. The guitar he played as a teenager gathered dust in the same garage he used to practice in, until eventually, it was sold or stashed in the attic (figuratively and literally).

So here you are, 25 years later. The lawyer/developer/marketer/care-taker, chained to your desk, your life duties, commitments, financial responsibilities and, perhaps, your childhood dreams. I ask you this: When was the last time you picked up a guitar? How would you feel if you bought yourself a new one, took lessons on YouTube, or formed a garage band with your buddies who feel the same way?

It's okay to nurture your decadent, ridiculous, childish whims! *Hello! Are you still in there?* Maybe you won't become the next Eddie Van Halen, but what about taking a few lessons? Sound ridiculous? *Fabulous!* It should! It will nurture your soul in a way you can't imagine and clearly haven't dared to dream of doing!

Perhaps when you go to work on Monday, you'll have a skip in your step or a smile on your face that just wasn't there before.

The goal here is to create balance, dig deep and tap into the things that give you a sense of accomplishment, satisfaction and stimulation. Find activities that simply make you happy while getting back in touch with your true self.

MATCH POINT

I just blew the dust off an old and cherished love of mine from childhood, and the part of my soul that was fueled by that love has been restored. In my case, instead of buying a new guitar, it was a tennis racquet.

When I was a little girl living in Australia, my dad played Jr. Wimbledon and Jr. Davis Cup against some of the big tennis greats. He understood the value and fun of the game — and his was old-school tennis: clay courts, tennis whites and wood rackets. Lucky for me, my parents instilled that love for tennis in us kids as well.

My sisters and I loved to play, and I took that much further. I always had a racquet in my hand, and, as we moved from country to country, tennis was my sanctuary, my "go-to place." It was a way to bond with new friends in new places with some common ground. I even got Jimmy Connors to sign my racquet cover when I met him in an airport when I was just a teenager. He was my rock star tennis idol, and meeting him was everything to me! I still have that racquet cover sitting in my bedroom as a reminder that tennis is one of my first great passions.

In high school, I chose cheerleading over the tennis team (yes, I'm admitting it!) but still played recreationally with friends and family through high school and college.

And then, I stopped. Just like that. Life got in the way.

When my boys were old enough, I got them on the court. It was a life skill, sport and passion I wanted them to have. When I started to play here and there with them, it reminded me how much I loved and missed the game. I vowed every time to pick it up again . . . but I didn't.

Again, life got in the way.

I had "tennis envy" of everyone who played. I still loved the game, but everything else seemed to take precedence. Plus, I had my hands full with other activities — Zumba, Pilates, Yoga, business commitments and my mom job.

Fast forward — my youngest son was an excellent player on the high school tennis team. When I asked him to play with me, he refused. He thought he was too good to bother with me. Hmmm — that got me going! So when my husband asked me to sign up for a tennis clinic with him, without hesitation, I said "Yes."

That first week, I played five times and hired a coach. I fully re-engaged in my first love, and I cannot even describe how incredible it feels to be reconnected to the game.

My scheduling priorities shifted from "I can't play tennis because I have a business dinner," to "I can't go to that business dinner because I'm playing tennis!" As a result, I've found many new tennis partners — business colleagues and friends — who now socialize over a game, rather than the traditional lunch, drinks or dinner plans. This is what dusting off those childhood passions is all about!

THE MAN WITH THE VIOLIN

Reinvention is our soul food. It rekindles our fire and renews our spirit.

There are innumerable small ways to transform our lives that impact the bigger picture. When we're open to the options — and even the challenges — they can truly change our spirit, mood and complete environment. We have the freedom to make these changes and Reinvent to our heart's content.

Wouldn't you like to take advantage of something that's just at your fingertips?

I met a man on a business trip a few years ago. A mutual friend introduced us in the gateway prior to boarding the plane. We were both headed to the same conference. Scott Neitlich had a large, rectangular case with him, and I asked him what was inside, assuming it was goodies for the conference. When he told me it was his violin and mentioned he "never went anywhere without it," I was intrigued.

Being the shy person I am, I drilled him with questions for the next 45 minutes on the short flight. He told me he had never played before in his life until recently but had always dreamed about it. A few years earlier, he went out and just bought a violin at a second hand store, downloaded video tutorials on YouTube, and taught himself how to play. Now he indulges in Debussy, Chopin, Tchaikovsky anytime and anywhere he pleases.

Scott brings his violin to the office every day. At lunchtime, he takes his violin to the park across the street and plays. When he's traveling, the hotels provide an empty meeting space or ballroom so he can play without disturbing the guests. There are no excuses and no limitations to making the time and place to practice and enjoy his violin.

"

DON'T WAIT TO DO THE THINGS YOU DREAM ABOUT.

Scott says:

"You have no idea how empowering playing the instrument is, and the fact that it is under my control. Working for large corporations and companies, my job has often been at the whim of the current stock price or a VP's attitude. Having the violin allowed me to have something that could not be taken away. I earned the knowledge myself, and, no matter what happened in my career or life, no one could/can take that away."

It feeds Scott's soul, so, he makes space for it in his life. As a matter of fact, the violin caused the mind-shift that gave him confidence to truly Reinvent his life and it's a big reason why he moved cross country and now works for himself in a product and branding consulting business.

With new patterns and awareness, you'll see new things stand out as they never have before. You're creating new space to see and experience new things. There's no need to deprive yourself of the things you want in this life. *Take baby steps to create your own happiness, and remember, it is never too late to try.*

I meet people every day in so many different walks of life and at so many levels of their careers — from 19-year-olds just starting out to retired 72-year-olds. They all speak from their different perspectives about what they wish they could do with their lives. The older folks who haven't fulfilled their dreams look at their lives and wish they'd done things differently. They question whether it's too late to tackle their dreams now.

We're living longer, more active and healthier lives than ever before. These factors enable us to have second and third chapters and multiple incarnations of our lives. Retirement is no longer a common next step after decades of work. You'll read a great story of a Serial Reinventor in Chapter 16. Ilene Sykes, who, in her later years of life, when many tend

"

WHEN WE LET OUR DREAMS GO,
WE LET PART OF OURSELVES
GO WITH THEM.

RE:INVENTION POWER TOOL

#5
THE BRAND NEW/OLD YOU "TO-DO" LIST

- **Go somewhere and daydream.**
  › Leave your phone at home, and let your mind wander.

- **Buy magazines of all sorts.**
  › Flip through them, and pull out anything that gets your attention: a headline, a chair, a wall color, a favorite shoe, a look, a font style, a profound statement.

- **Collect things that excite or interest you.**

- **Do you see a pattern or any similarities?**

- **Is there anything that inspires a "Maybe I could/should" thought?**

- **Repeat the same exercise again a few weeks later.**

These suggestions help you focus on the things you love by bringing them to the forefront of your mind. Why shouldn't you have them?

- **Want more sunshine? Go outside!**

- **Like music? Turn it on!**

- **Craving some food? Go get it!**

- **Miss seeing people? Invite them into your life more!**

- **Love your work? Do more of it!**

- **Longing for leisure time? Create it!**

to retire, was just getting revved up on yet another new career. She's having the time of her life, running circles around her peers in the business!

Many people of retirement age are moving into entrepreneurship or returning to the work force to stay stimulated and engaged. Or they're discovering their long-buried passions and hobbies, thus setting a wonderful and inspired example to their grandkids. They're showing the younger generations all the possibilities that life has to offer at any stage.

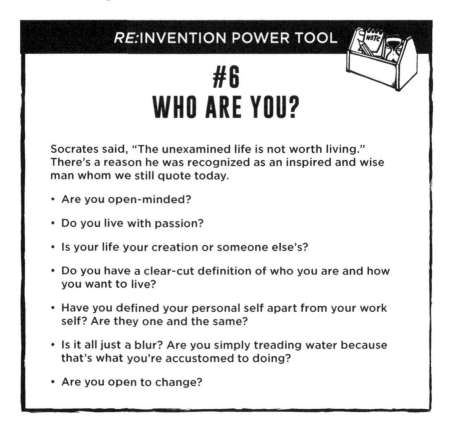

*RE:*INVENTION POWER TOOL

#6
WHO ARE YOU?

Socrates said, "The unexamined life is not worth living." There's a reason he was recognized as an inspired and wise man whom we still quote today.

- Are you open-minded?

- Do you live with passion?

- Is your life your creation or someone else's?

- Do you have a clear-cut definition of who you are and how you want to live?

- Have you defined your personal self apart from your work self? Are they one and the same?

- Is it all just a blur? Are you simply treading water because that's what you're accustomed to doing?

- Are you open to change?

"When I was five years old, my mother always told me that happiness was the key to life. When I went to school, they asked me what I wanted to be when I grew up. I wrote down 'happy.' They told me I didn't understand the assignment. I told them they didn't understand life."

— John Lennon

CHANGE: FEAR OR ADVENTURE?

In my life, change was always an adventure. Throughout my childhood, we moved to three different countries and had to start over in new neighborhoods and with new friends, schools and surroundings. I loved it and took on each move with curiosity, a sense of exploration and an interest to build the next place in my life. It gave me the tools to appreciate new things and get to know something or someone from the beginning.

I was a student of the world and exposed to all the diversities of life, races, religions, classes — it's the fabric of me — all woven together. When tackling a new project, client, hobby, friendship, I embrace it with this attitude. Not everyone has the same feeling about change and Reinvention. The unknown can be a little daunting, but I encourage you to look at the rewards, the upside and the potential outcome.

Take baby steps to get there. Huge leaps aren't necessary. If you're just procrastinating, *try not to let your TO-DOs get in the way of your WHAT IFs! Spread your wings, and embrace the beauty and excitement of "newness."*

If you find something you love to do, with the same sense of wonder and exploration you experienced as a kid, you'll *love* what you do with your life. Take it from someone who knows. After 30 years of loving what I do, I'm still Reinventing every day.

STAND IN YOUR TRUTH

That being said, we're all a work in progress. My friend James Damian acknowledges it's something we all need to be conscious of. He's a big advocate for being true to yourself, your passions and your spirit. These personal hallmarks have been his anchor through a long and fascinating career as an innovator. They've allowed him to trust the creative process and create new opportunities and relationships. This philosophy has taken him from the retail windows on 5th Avenue to the boardroom as chairman of a public company.

James has always had the ability to live in the ambiguity of not having all the answers or knowing what's around each corner. He thinks the Internet Age has allowed for broader creativity because it has eliminated the middleman in a number of industries: music, film, design, photography and writing. The age barrier is less of an issue now than it was before, as we have the access to tools for continual self-expression and co-creation. *"Culture is key, and leaders must stand at the intersection of humanity and commerce,"* says James.

After 12 years as Chief Design Officer at Best Buy, James made the decision to move on. It was at a time when the company was thriving, due in large part to his visionary leadership and passion for the customer experience.

There were many factors that led to this next evolution. When he joined the company, they were looking for someone who could build, design and foster innovation at the company. He was able to iterate new concepts so they could position themselves ahead of the competition. The freedom he was given was like a spark plug for him.

But as the years went by, as is so often the case with size and success, the company had less room for flexibility for exploration. This was due to the complacency often associated with success coupled with a change at the CEO level. James learned that design leaders need to have sponsorship from both the board and the CEO to create a "Design Culture," or it would not be sustainable.

Ultimately, there wasn't enough for him to hold onto at the company. James says:

> "You need to know what's right for you and follow your heart. I wanted to be a leader who would constantly inspire and motivate others to look at the big picture from a broader perspective.
>
> This comes from investigating your higher purpose: who you are versus what you do. Many people lose sight of who they are along the way.
>
> By understanding your higher purpose, you will elevate your whole being. You reach a level of distinction. I've always been a dreamer, curious about what's possible, and I've always had an inner restlessness. When I was at Best Buy, I was deeply connected to the work I was doing — so much so that 12 years went by."

Soon after he left Best Buy and launched James Damian's Brand Integration Services, his wife was diagnosed with breast cancer. The couple took stock and identified the activities and commitments that were clogging their precious time. What could they edit out to emphasize the things that were most important to them? They both wanted to focus on doing only things they loved.

For James, the experience enabled him to concentrate on board work with the Minnesota Orchestra and at a small, nimble growth company. He says these opportunities allow him to give more of himself and be of better use to people who want to do good. He also now has more time with his best advisor and friend, Debra, his wife of 37 years, and their three children. These conscious decisions amount to James's ability to stand in his truth and participate in the things in his life that truly matter.

By knowing himself and remaining true to what drives him, James has shown that yes, he's still in there! His passions may have shifted through the years, but the overriding themes have been consistent: design, innovation, balance, exploration, curiosity, creativity and working from a constant state of empathy.

James always closes his workshops and keynotes with this quote: *"I have learned that people will forget what you said, people will forget what you did, but people will never forget how you made them feel."*

— Maya Angelou

So, summon the courage to explore the *you* that you want to be. Are you allowing yourself the time to indulge your joy and nurture your soul? Give yourself the permission and the space to let it in, and, little by little, it will take over the parts that you were holding back. Be adventurous with yourself — maybe at first it's just an idea or thought that you allow to manifest. Make a date to reflect, act and Reinvent!

CHAPTER 4:

THE BALANCING ACT

"The most confused you will ever get is when you try to convince
your heart and spirit of something your mind knows is a lie."
— Shannon L. Adler

Long ago — before I had children — in fact, before I was even married, I read an article that hit me hard. It was about priorities. The article stated that human beings are capable of effectively managing *three* priorities in life at any given time. *Three!* If we try to do more, we'll end up faltering on all of them.

Three has always been an important number to me. I come from a family of three girls. I've lived in three countries. Growing up, I had two best friends (we were the Three Musketeers as far back as I can remember them). I have three boys (two sons and one husband). The concept of choosing three things to prioritize felt almost spiritual to me.

Still, as a successful businesswoman, I had far more than three priorities in my life. Probably more than ten! And that doesn't even include family, fitness or any of the other things I'm supposed to work on every day to be happy and healthy.

Fast forward 30+ years, and life is certainly no simpler than it used to be. Choosing three priorities still seems impossible. Most people aren't able to limit themselves to three social media accounts, let alone three total life priorities. And yet — if curiosity is an act of self-care, which I firmly believe it is — we owe it to ourselves to explore what those three life priorities might be, especially if we feel less than stellar about our current situation.

After all, some of us are happy in our marriages but feel uninspired at work. Others dream of a more fulfilling love life but are completely in tune on the work front. Still, some of us feel a quiet tug for a bit more excitement in life, while others feel the need to stage a complete mutiny.

Whatever the case, the only way to answer the yearning is to get up close with *you* — the *real* you — and determine what lights you up . . . what sets you off . . . what will bring your life into a more divine expression. Let's get started.

IDENTIFY YOUR PRIORITIES

Take your time as you digest and consider what is truly most important to you. I invite you to drill down a bit further.

For instance:

- "Family" can mean many things. Children. Husband. Aging parents. Little sisters or brothers. Sick relatives. Each requires different kinds of work and love to keep your relationships strong and healthy.

- "Love" can also mean many things. It could mean dating, self-love or even working through some childhood traumas to get back to a more peaceful and healthy you. It could mean creating

*RE:*INVENTION POWER TOOL

#7
WHAT MAKES YOU HAPPY?

Making lists is a huge part of Reinvention. We started in Chapter 1 by making a list of whenever you felt happy, and I invite you again, to make a list of your current priorities — the areas you would like to give the maximum amount of time and energy. Don't limit yourself to choosing just three (yet).

Open up your mind, and brainstorm all of the areas in your life you would like to give more attention.

The following are a few ideas to get you started. Feel free to add on to the list:

Love	Hobbies
Family	Emotional Wellness
Friendships	Finances
Career	Downtime
Spirituality	Creative Expression
Health and Fitness	Sex
Diet	Independence
Fashion	Meditation
Home Décor	Sleep
Self-Exploration	Charity/Community
Travel	

a loving consciousness, being more connected, giving back to your community, making love the core of your existence.

- "Fitness" is more than just exercise. It's eating healthfully — mindfulness — living a stronger, more centered and active life.

The trick to this exercise is finding what it means *to you*.

Tell the truth: Did you just say to yourself, "This is a good idea. I'll do it later," kept reading, answered it in your head and moved on? Most likely! Guess what? That's exactly what we do all the time, and that's why we don't actually make changes.

Put this book down, go get a piece of paper and pen, and take 10 minutes to do this exercise. Go on. Really . . . now . . .

.

.

.

.

Ah, that's it!

You're taking an important step toward Reinventing your life.

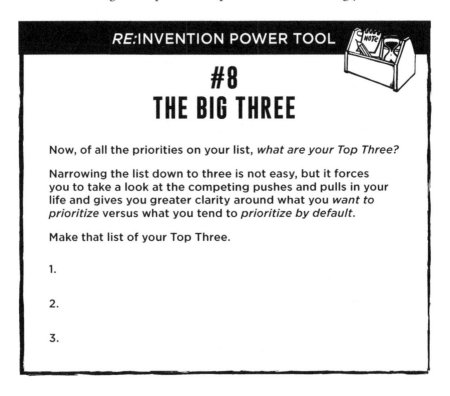

RE:INVENTION POWER TOOL

#8
THE BIG THREE

Now, of all the priorities on your list, *what are your Top Three?*

Narrowing the list down to three is not easy, but it forces you to take a look at the competing pushes and pulls in your life and gives you greater clarity around what you *want to prioritize* versus what you tend to *prioritize by default.*

Make that list of your Top Three.

1.

2.

3.

*"Most of us spend too much time on what is urgent
and not enough time on what is important."*

— Stephen R. Covey

DIG DEEPER

- What surprised you about your top-three priorities?

- Was it harder or easier than you expected to narrow your priority list to three things?

- Do your daily activities truly support these top-three priorities? If not, what could you be doing differently?

Consider how the decisions you make each day support your "Top-Three" — or not. What steps can you take to bring your life into better alignment?

If setting a more fulfilling career in motion is one of your most important priorities, then you should allocate your time to that great mission. If forming more meaningful relationships with your children is one of your top-three priorities, then you need to devote time to nurturing those relationships.

The problem many of us face in this frenetic world is that much of our energy is devoted to areas outside of our "Top Three" priority triangle, which takes us ever further from our true, purposeful path.

WHAT'S GOTTA GIVE

My amazing friend since college, Lisa Licht, former CMO of Live Nation, told me that for her, "Reinvention is a constant state of mind."

She recently spoke about her "Packing Your Suitcase" approach to building her professional path in life for an article on *Forbes.com*.

Lisa always sought jobs where she would be challenged and acquire new skills — skills she brought with her to her new jobs. From Mattel to 20th Century Fox, to Hasbro, to Yahoo, to Live Nation, she was very deliberate about her choices, often choosing positions that would add to her "suitcase" of life experience over promotions and titles. *Lisa says that the theme of her story is flexibility and insatiable curiosity.*

> "I started realizing that, if I had skills nobody else had, it gave me a competitive edge that separated me from the pack. That's when I started thinking of my professional life as similar to packing a suitcase. When traveling, I try to be deliberate and efficient, packing the most unique pieces. The same mindset applies to learning skills. You want to consciously acquire skills that make you a dynamic leader and propel you closer to your goals.
>
> The benefits of the suitcase framework are twofold. By approaching your professional goals from a holistic perspective, you can structure your life towards developing the skills you need to achieve them. Your focus on acquiring a diverse set of skills not only expands your career prospects; through leveraging them, you become a multifaceted addition to every team you join. As the breadth of insight and capabilities in your suitcase increases, so does the magnitude of your opportunities."

Despite her career success, Lisa didn't always have the same level of balance between home and work that she enjoys today. She told me her biggest Ah-Ha Moment came when her daughter was just a few months old, and she was working late at the office (again).

Her husband, Andy, called her at work and asked why she wanted to have a family at all if she was never going to be home. He was (and still is) extremely supportive of her career track, but he knew she could be successful without working 13 hours a day and sacrificing the needs of her family in the process. He firmly pointed out that professional success was not worth missing their kids' childhoods for. He was right.

Lisa listened when her husband suggested she revisit her priorities. Ever since that phone call, she made it a point to be home in time for dinner five nights a week. This left her one night for work functions and Saturdays for a date night with Andy. She didn't have much time left over for her friends, but we understood she was trying to balance her career and family, and we supported her commitment to both.

Realizing that it's okay to have (sometimes) competing priorities helped Lisa to carve out time to take care of her family's needs as well as her responsibilities at work, proving it can be done. *You don't necessarily have to sacrifice one priority for the sake of another. You simply have to be conscientious about what amount of energy goes where and if that distribution is working for your life.*

It was truly remarkable what Lisa managed to juggle into her life. She had a clear and dedicated commitment to both her family and her career. With significant jobs over the last three decades, Lisa continued to be "all in" with every role and task she undertook, and she was revered as a great leader, manager, colleague and friend. Her focus and dedication have led her to a place in her life where she truly gets to call the shots. She's carved out a wonderful consulting business . . . until her next Reinvention comes along.

"Only I can change my life. No one can do it for me."

— Carol Burnett

GUT CHECK

In order for life to be truly fulfilling, our actions and priorities must align with our values. For instance, when we spend a lot of time doing things that don't resonate with us — things that don't allow us to see our values in a meaningful way — we become frustrated and unhappy.

Unfortunately, this is a reality for so many of us. We spend our days slaving away at the office for jobs we don't care about — coaching or carpooling for a multitude of our children's activities — socializing with people we no longer feel a connection to, or attending events that have no meaning for us. *True harmony is achieved when your priorities, actions and values are in alignment.*

Part of assessing your life to determine if you could benefit from a Reinvention means asking yourself the tough questions — and giving the tough and honest answers. *The only wrong answer is a dishonest one.*

We've already started the question-and-answer process in the very first chapter, but Reinvention requires an ongoing assessment. Indeed, introspection will be your closest companion on this Reinvention journey.

Take a few moments to dig deep and answer the questions in the exercise. They are designed to help you identify what you value. Allow yourself grace. Let go of self-judgment, and don't worry what others would think of your answers. It's not *their* life you're saving.

My friend Bob's decision to leave Wall Street and go back to school was the result of these kinds of tough questions — and so was his decision to keep pursuing that route, even when life (with mounting student debt and a much lower salary) was not easy. The situation forced him to look at his values and what truly made him happy.

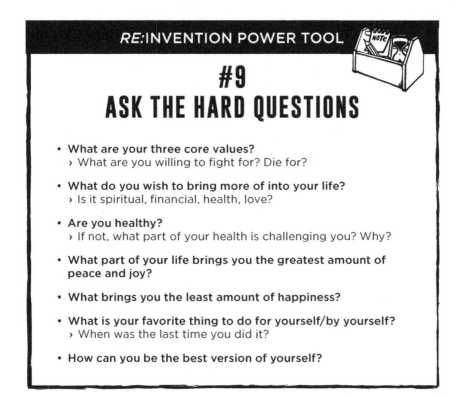

RE:INVENTION POWER TOOL

#9
ASK THE HARD QUESTIONS

- **What are your three core values?**
  › What are you willing to fight for? Die for?

- **What do you wish to bring more of into your life?**
  › Is it spiritual, financial, health, love?

- **Are you healthy?**
  › If not, what part of your health is challenging you? Why?

- **What part of your life brings you the greatest amount of peace and joy?**

- **What brings you the least amount of happiness?**

- **What is your favorite thing to do for yourself/by yourself?**
  › When was the last time you did it?

- **How can you be the best version of yourself?**

Reinvention requires a day-to-day gut check and forces you to create your own personal definition of success. For Bob, that meant being open to a complete "value shift." He says:

> "I had been disillusioned with my prior career, as well as with my relationships, buying into the conventional ideas of what 'success' and 'happiness' were. It was only through this experience that I was able to see people I admired and respected live a different life, an engaged life, and I really, really wanted what they had."

> *"You have to maintain a culture of transformation and stay true to your values."*
> — Jeff Weiner, CEO, LinkedIn

CHAPTER 5

PUT YOURSELF FIRST

"It's not selfish to love yourself, take care of yourself and to make your happiness a priority. It's necessary."
— Mandy Hale

If *you* are not at the very top of your priority list from the previous chapter, we've got a problem. Focus, get clear and put yourself first. Once you create true focus around your end goal, you'll be amazed at how clear the moving pieces will become.

SAVE YOURSELF

When Maureen Barten was diagnosed with blood cancer, it forced her to take a hard look at her life. At a time when many would hunker down and simply try to get through the crisis, Maureen realized there were many areas in her life that she was unhappy about. One of those was in her marriage.

On the eve of her first round of chemotherapy, she knew that *no amount of drugs would fix the sadness, anger and desperate loneliness she was living with. She needed to deal with the real issue — her aching heart.*

Many years earlier, Maureen's mother advised her, "Mo, whatever happens in life, no matter how difficult, you *must* save yourself first. If you do not endure, your children will suffer badly." She replayed her mother's words and, in autopilot mode, did what she had to do to save herself.

During one particularly brutal argument with her husband, Maureen seized the moment to set herself free. There was no flutter of nerves. No anxiousness. No fear. Just resolve, self-respect and, actually, relief. She left her marriage of nearly 20 years. Initially, she left her 14- and 16-year-old sons, too. She left everything except her clothes and a bit of crockery.

Through her sickness, her treatment, her sons' individual ordeals, and the wreckage of her marriage, Maureen learned to find herself — long lost in an emotionally challenging marriage — by putting herself first. Amidst the mayhem, she reconnected with who she had always been by harnessing her own strength in order to identify, set and enforce boundaries: first with herself, then with her children and then with the rest of the world.

She learned to listen more and speak less. She learned to accept help and how to ask for it, too. Out of the ashes, Maureen's life was transformed. She actively (and painfully) ushered the negativity out of her life — and in so doing, welcomed a new world of good.

THE IMPORTANCE OF BEING SELFISH, AKA SELF-CARE

We spend a good part of our lives tending to others, in service of those we love or work for. In relationships, we often adapt or sacrifice our own wants and needs for those we love. As a result, we may not tend to ourselves with the same care and attention we give to those around us.

You may feel you're not entitled to your own desires, and that's just so wrong. If you don't take care of yourself, who will? Before you embark on this new Reinvention chapter of your life, I'm here to grant you the permission to be "selfish" and go for it.

Because . . .

- *Self-time* is not selfish

- *Self-empowerment* is not arrogant

- *Indulgence* is necessary

- *Self-entitlement* is fundamental

But wait . . . you can't abandon your kids, your spouse, the people who love you and need you with reckless abandon! You likely have dependents, and it may not be fair, right or appropriate to jump on a plane and disappear for three months to Australia, an Ashram or on a European bike tour. I'm not advocating you run away and never look back, but you can (and should) put yourself first always, just as Maureen's mother advised her to do.

> *"You have something unique that no one else has — your life experience. That's the power of you."*
> — Mel Robbins

If you find yourself living a life that's not quite what you signed up for, take stock and remind yourself: it is *your* life. With a little planning and consideration, you actually can put your own needs first!

You may feel you're not *entitled* to do what you dream about. You sit and watch the world go by, while friends and colleagues live out their dreams. From the sidelines, you say, "Why can't I?" or "I could never do that" or "I have too many responsibilities. My spouse would never let me. My mother needs 24–7 care. I can't leave. The kids are too young." Get the picture?

I heard a quote recently that reminded me of something we've heard often enough, but it bears repeating: *"Don't count on others to fulfill us; it is only we who can fulfill ourselves."*

Therefore, think about all the wonderful things you want to explore, incorporate them into your life and own them. Your balance and passion will be much greater as a result.

Often times, we feel like the weight of the world is solely on our shoulders — that we don't deserve to make time for ourselves or to place our happiness in front of someone else's. *Part of your journey will involve recognizing the worth of both your dreams* and *yourself.*

PROJECT YOU

If you truly want to put yourself first, you'll have to exercise some personal *tough love* and make time for "Project *You.*"

First, you need to believe you are *entitled* to your own happiness. With one subtle mind shift, you can put all the right pieces in place to create the life you want. It's okay to be self-caring (aka selfish) and look out for yourself.

When you "put your own oxygen mask on first" — as the airlines say — you serve yourself and those around you better. When you are strong of fortitude and direction — confident in your ability to take care of yourself, and happier as a result — everyone else will most definitely benefit. *So, dare to dream, dare to be indulgent, dare to feel entitled and dare to live greatly!*

"

ONCE YOU HAVE A PLAN,
BREAK IT INTO SECTIONS AND
GET SPECIFIC. THE MORE DETAILED
YOU ARE, THE MORE CLARITY
YOU'LL HAVE AROUND EACH PIECE,
AND THE EASIER IT WILL BE TO
FIGURE OUT HOW TO BRIDGE YOUR
ENTIRE VISION TOGETHER.

But, as we all well know, saying (or reading) and doing are two entirely different things. To get started in daring greatly:

- Treat your own life as you would a client if you were a consultant

- Have a real conversation with yourself (on paper is preferred), and take yourself seriously

- Set up appointments with yourself to work on your Reinvention Road Map (detailed thoroughly in Chapter 17)

- Create a task list/agenda for each meeting so you have milestones to reach for your short- and long-term plan

When you treat yourself the same way you treat your other obligations — your boss, your spouse, your kids, even your friends when they need you — the things you care about will get addressed today instead of "someday." *Someday* is here now, so dig deep, and think about what you want. Even the smallest changes affect your core being, your level of happiness, your ability to smile on the inside, and, thus, the outside will *shine*.

GO INTO THE QUIET

Have you ever noticed that your greatest ideas and life-shattering epiphanies seem to come during moments of calm? Perhaps they come to you when taking a shower, strolling along on a nice walk, or lying down for a quick catnap. That's because we need headspace for new ideas to happen!

Start with five minutes a day, and work up to ten or fifteen. The longer you allow yourself time to rest and reflect, the more time your heart will have to speak to your mind and determine your next course of action. Another, more structured option? Meditation.

Never tried meditating? That's OK. There is literally no wrong way to do it. It doesn't matter if you feel silly or crazy or can't clear your "monkey brain" for more than a few seconds at a time when you first get started. Tons of websites feature guided meditations to help you clear your consciousness and allow inspiring thoughts to come through. Give it a try! See what this new "door" will open.

LISTEN TO YOUR HEART

Matt Hanover spent most of his life avoiding the quiet. He's the first to admit he "listened to his head over his heart." Matt had been charging hard since he'd been a young boy. A consummate child entrepreneur, he started the "Willy Wonka Candy Factory" in elementary school. Through his school years, he was a magician. Matt started writing marketing materials at the age of 11. By 12, he had an answering machine and the vanity phone number 88-MAGIC.

His ability to turn ideas into money-making opportunities continued through college after the Mac and laser printer were invented. He started an off-campus, monthly, ad-supported newspaper and made enough money to cover his last two years of tuition. Simultaneously he interned for an entertainment PR and Marketing Agency.

Post-graduation, Matt zig-zagged across the country, devoting his seemingly boundless energy and intelligence to the growth of well-known blue-chip companies: Turner Broadcasting, Yahoo, DIRECTV and IMDb/Amazon. Between those jobs, he had his own consulting business and a dotcom start-up. He took risks, lost savings, made deals, reorganized processes, negotiated and managed relationships, constantly shape-shifting from one company to the next.

"

YOU MUST MAKE SPACE FOR NEW GOOD TO FIND YOU.

Matt experienced peak career moments such as meeting Malcolm Forbes (who gave him a tour of his Faberge eggs) and doing deals with Don King, the Rolling Stones and Tom Petty. Despite the incredible opportunities and perks, Matt always had a yearning to do something else. One of Wayne Dyer's questions nagged at the back of his mind: *What if you get to the end of your life and you haven't sung the song that's inside of you?*

He took a few sabbaticals from building other people's dreams along the way, but, ultimately, it was a panic attack (which felt like a heart attack) that led Matt to think about making some serious life changes.

Those thoughts were reinforced when he was nearly simultaneously diagnosed with chronic lymphocytic leukemia and thyroid cancer. Following surgery for removing his thyroid, his vocal nerve was damaged, and he literally had no voice for six months.

Matt left his career path and pursued a graduate degree in spiritual psychology. In the program, he was encouraged to declare for himself whatever he wanted to be — assuming fear was not a consideration and it was 50% believable. He declared himself an artist. With no formal training and only painting as a quiet hobby, he posted several of his pieces on Facebook to let his friends know of his intention. Over the course of the next seven years, Matt reorganized his life around his health and making art—then found projects he could do to support himself. Making this shift to emphasizing what he loves has made a huge difference, he says.

Matt's changes were dramatic and difficult. He battled internal fears, and still does, around his art not being "good enough." He now knows when he starts a new painting, there's a roller coaster coming. He starts with enthusiasm before quickly going downhill, which involves hating the piece, questioning every decision in his life and hearing prior negative words from teachers, friends and strangers — right before a glimmer of hope. Then there would be another glimmer, and, ultimately, he would "find" the painting he was hoping to make.

On his fears, Matt says:

"For me, I'm not trying to conquer fear, anxiety or 'enough-ness' anymore. I've learned in psychology class that these are all characters in my dramatic play, and I give them a voice. If I can just allow myself to feel those things and still take the next right action, a three-foot toss forward, then I can get there. I have the sense-memory now of working through them.

I didn't have a concrete plan or a large financial runway in place to become a full-time artist. I admire the many artists who do it. I had to surrender the need for stability and trust this would work out, despite days when there was absolutely no evidence of that being true.

My version of a 'Reinvention' was an exercise in listening to my heart, managing my head and putting my health first. I have tried *not* taking care of myself a number of times, and it still doesn't work. I've had to learn to access my higher wisdom at the expense of my ego. Having a big job and driving a Mercedes was very cool. It was a lot of fun. Eating a pint of ice cream every day after work to quell my anxiety was not."

The experience of embracing fear as part of the journey has been a surprise. His psychology degree gave him a framework to better understand his life and circumstances, but, like everyone, he is prone to spirals of self-recrimination. When those moments come, he has to "throw paint, dance, sing (off-key) and practice gratitude to return to joy."

As we can see, self-care and a sense of entitlement can go a long way and help pull us out of those situations that can spiral. It may seem difficult, but the moment you start to do the work, even if in baby steps, you'll inch towards the right direction that will bring you the fulfilment you're seeking. It's better than the alternative, and you'll be surprised at what shows up along your journey. Just allow it.

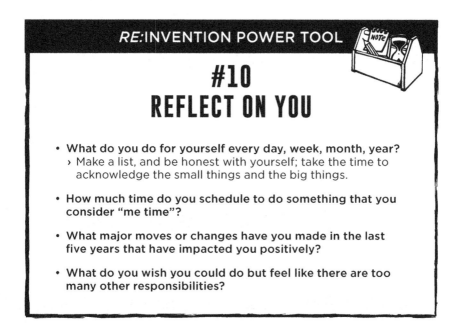

*RE:*INVENTION POWER TOOL

#10
REFLECT ON YOU

- **What do you do for yourself every day, week, month, year?**
  › Make a list, and be honest with yourself; take the time to acknowledge the small things and the big things.

- **How much time do you schedule to do something that you consider "me time"?**

- **What major moves or changes have you made in the last five years that have impacted you positively?**

- **What do you wish you could do but feel like there are too many other responsibilities?**

PART 2:
THE WORK

CHAPTER 6:

THE COURAGE TO *RE:*INVENT — FIGHT THE FEAR

"Fear is a reaction. Courage is a decision."
— Winston Churchill

A small dose of courage helps with Reinvention. Do you have it?

Where does one find the courage to make a change? Change requires a great leap of faith to define and explore your wants and needs. When you understand that you need a change or have merely entertained the thought, the first reaction is usually fear — fear of the unknown.

Reality of some sort sets in, and you quickly negate the notion that change is in the cards. You play the same mantra over and over in your head. You come up with the same excuses, and you rationalize all the reasons why you can't pursue that dream, passion, relationship, career or goal. Maybe old stories and habits are running you, and you've not managed to rewire your connection to "change." But what is *really* stopping you?

*"Courage is the most important of all the virtues,
because without courage, you can't practice any other
virtue consistently. You can practice any virtue erratically,
but nothing consistently without courage."*

— Maya Angelou

IF AT FIRST, YOU DON'T SUCCEED — TRY, TRY AGAIN

There's absolutely no reason you can't create the life you want. It may take time, dedication and focus, but you can control all of this and block fear from getting in the way. What may seem daunting or unachievable is yours with each and every step you take towards it. Every little step is a major milestone and a reason to celebrate — with a pat on the back, a glass of wine, a victory dance — it's yours, so own it!

Beth Comstock, author of *Imagine It Forward: Courage, Creativity, and the Power of Change*, is a perfect example. She is a change-maker. Her mission is to understand what's next, navigate change and help people and organizations do the same. By cultivating the habit of seeking out new ideas, people and places, she built a career path from storyteller to Chief Marketer to GE Vice Chair.

In nearly three decades at GE, she led efforts to accelerate new growth and innovation, initiated GE's digital and clean-energy trans-formation, developed new businesses and enhanced GE's brand value and inventive culture.

Beth is a director at Nike, trustee of The National Geographic Society and former board president of the Cooper Hewitt Smithsonian National Design Museum. She graduated from the College of William and Mary with a degree in biology.

She has an impressive bio. Judging from it, we might assume that Beth has always been completely and utterly without fear, ready to make sweeping corporate changes without a moment's hesitation. Well, we would be wrong.

Beth used to be scared of change. She was shy and introverted and lacked confidence. She worried she was not good enough or prepared enough to succeed. *She knew her fears were irrational, but, still, they held her back because she believed them.*

Her awakening came after the birth of her first daughter, when she decided to become a single mother. She was a good girl from a small town, and she realized she was living her life according to other people's narratives instead of her own. Making the choice to leave her marriage and raise her daughter alone unearthed the courage she needed to shape her own future and pave her own path.

She knew her shyness was holding her back from engaging with others. She didn't like to speak up in meetings or nurture relationships with people who could have helped her move forward.

Beth had to face her fears head-on, but it didn't happen overnight. She did it by pushing ahead and making incremental changes. She took baby steps by giving herself small challenges: meet one person, ask one question, share one idea, then two, and so on. Facing her fears meant making behavioral changes.

"Try getting comfortable with change. Embrace it with excitement and courage. Minimize the fear, and let inspiration and curiosity take over."
— Beth Comstock

The biggest challenge she faced was the first step: admitting that *not changing* was holding her back. Her advice to anyone in a similar situation is *Just start. There is never a perfect time, and you will never have enough of what you think you need.*

Things got easier when she started to see positive results. She says:

"I'm incredibly proud of the connections I've made and the people I've been able to learn from — I feel very rich in this sense. And it is something that might not have happened if I had just gone with my natural ways.

I'm reinventing again, after a 30-year career. I had another 'divorce' of sorts when I left GE. I was ready to leave, but, at the same time, I have a new appreciation that change is hard — even for a change-maker."

We all know someone who is "stuck" and constantly sharing (aka complaining) about how miserable they are with something or someone. It's usually fear that stops them from confronting it head-on and figuring out how to move on. But really, what is "fear"? Fear is in our imagination, and it is a choice. We're telling ourselves a story. It's not real. It's what we make it. It's only as strong as the power and the voice you give it.

My friend Maureen says:

"Anger is a mask for fear. By the time I left my marriage, I was not afraid any longer. I learned that fear is imaginary. It is unknown, and so we make it ugly, or big, or a monster. But really, as it is unknown, maybe it's nothing at all! I suppose you could say I conquered my fear by learning that it was make-believe and by *understanding* and believing that it was just make-believe."

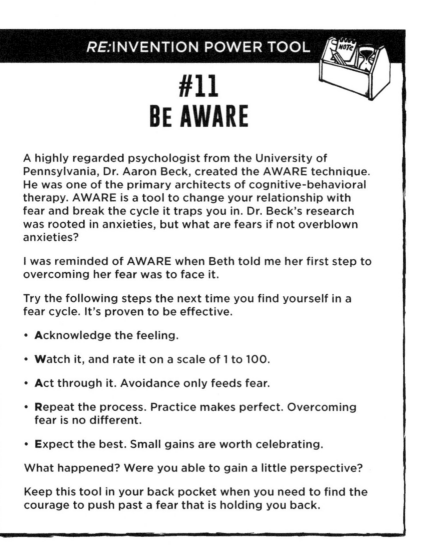

*RE:*INVENTION POWER TOOL

#11
BE AWARE

A highly regarded psychologist from the University of Pennsylvania, Dr. Aaron Beck, created the AWARE technique. He was one of the primary architects of cognitive-behavioral therapy. AWARE is a tool to change your relationship with fear and break the cycle it traps you in. Dr. Beck's research was rooted in anxieties, but what are fears if not overblown anxieties?

I was reminded of AWARE when Beth told me her first step to overcoming her fear was to face it.

Try the following steps the next time you find yourself in a fear cycle. It's proven to be effective.

- **A**cknowledge the feeling.

- **W**atch it, and rate it on a scale of 1 to 100.

- **A**ct through it. Avoidance only feeds fear.

- **R**epeat the process. Practice makes perfect. Overcoming fear is no different.

- **E**xpect the best. Small gains are worth celebrating.

What happened? Were you able to gain a little perspective?

Keep this tool in your back pocket when you need to find the courage to push past a fear that is holding you back.

DIG DEEPER

- How can you give so much power to something that is not real?

- How can your journey, dreams, passions and life fantasies not be more powerful than fear?

- Is the risk of daring and possibility of failing not worth the reward?

- How can you reward yourself as you overcome each obstacle?

- How truly risky is that change and Reinvention you want to explore?

"If it doesn't scare you, you're probably not dreaming big enough."
— Tori Burch

REJECTION: REFRAME YOUR BRAIN

I've had to apply these techniques for 30 years in my agency business and have taught the same to everyone who has worked with us. The PR, marketing and sponsorship business requires a lot of outreach, cold calling, presentations, sales pitches and creative-idea presentations that need to be sold. Each instance requires a mindset that can tolerate rejection.

Thirty years may have toughened me up, but the old sales adages still get me through: "No" means "maybe," and "I don't think so" means "there's wiggle room," so go for it. The saying, "Every 'no' is one step closer to a 'yes'" makes me jump up with delight. When someone tells me they're not interested, I celebrate because it means I can cross that company off the list and move on to someone else who is better suited for the partnership and client.

Sometimes we are hesitant to take a first step towards our dream or goal for fear of failure or rejection by others. We have an idea what others may not agree with or support, and, if we believe in it, we should learn to overcome the negativity when others don't get it — who cares? This is your life, not theirs! If they don't dare to dream or go for their goals and create their own greatest life, that's their loss; it's certainly not your concern.

Find that one champion — other than that great voice in your head that's nagging for you to "go for it" — and that's all you need. My sister Carolynn is that champion. Ever since I was little, not to mention born on *her* birthday two years later — thus her real-life birthday present (or so I like to think) — she's been the one to inspire me, show me what perseverance and focus get you, reminds me on the tough days what I'm good at, encourages me to dream and create. She's my biggest supporter and champion and often my "go to" when I need just that little boost — and yes, we all do need that!

Many women of my generation were not taught to be persistent when they were growing up. Consequently, they didn't learn how to deal with rejection and forge ahead despite it, in search of the next interaction, meeting, partner or goal. Some say it has to do with the "dating/mating" rituals of yesteryear, when women waited for invitations and were not vocal about their needs. We were socialized and educated differently than men, so we require a little more conscious awareness and training to manage and compartmentalize the negative associations of rejection, to overcome them and to have a voice that is heard.

"I've always been comfortable being uncomfortable and willing to go where others have been afraid to go — whether that's been pioneering online research or going into the business of equality," says Shelley Zalis, CEO of The Female Quotient, and Founder of The Girls Lounge.

She goes on to say, "Everything I do is not in a textbook, so I have to create the new norm. I call my Ah-Ha Moments 'heartbeat' moments. These were times when my heart was pounding, and I knew I had to listen to my heart. For example, I was at a market-research company, and I had the idea to migrate research from offline to online. I was told that it wasn't the right time, and no one was online except for affluent men with broadband connections. I decided to make it the right moment and create a new ecosystem."

It turned out to be an extremely successful venture! Shelley has been able to show how the "power of the pack," in what seems to have been a male-dominated world, is a powerful initiative. Whether it's walking the floor at CES or taking on major gender and pay-equality issues in corporate America, she's bringing women's voices to the global stage and creating impact and change.

Shelley's greatest fear was *not* doing something. "We all have self-doubt, but you have to shut off that negative voice in your head. Arianna Huffington calls that voice in our heads the 'obnoxious roommate.' My mom always taught me that confidence is beautiful and that you have to believe in yourself first before anyone else can," says Shelley.

She says, "I don't just re-invent, I invent anew. My advice would be to believe in yourself. Own what makes you different, because that is what makes you unique.

"Also, don't think the world will change overnight, because it's not that black-and-white. Nuance is what makes businesses unique and special. If I tried to create what I created, I wouldn't have created it. There is no road map for innovation. When you're creating out of the box, you have to create a new box and make it up as you go along."

Shelley's definition of success is "one who is wealthy is one who is happy with what she has. I don't think of success in monetary terms but in terms of being happy with my work." She is inspiring men and women all over the world to be their best selves, and she leads by example.

Dealing with a fear of rejection comes down to how we frame things in our own minds, as opposed to using society's norms as a benchmark.

When you go in search of rejection or disappointment, your response won't be as negative as it would be if you expect a "Yes" at every turn because you're "expecting" it.

Toss those "No's" aside, and use them as stepping stones to get to the place you want to be — the place you're meant to be. It's how you choose to frame those moments — be it an external force or an internal emotion. *You will always have control over fear of rejection if you learn to frame your internal and external responses to them.* Others' negativity will become a catalyst for your own accomplishments.

EMOTIONAL RESCUE

Our emotions — both good and bad — are huge indicators of how we feel about our lives, even beyond the obvious question: "How does your life make you feel right now?" Our reactions to everyday occurrences are windows into our heart. They allow us to get a better pulse on the things we've been pushing into our subconscious because they're too difficult to deal with directly.

For instance, if you find yourself feeling joyful and "getting lost" each time you work on a new art project, this is a sign that art is healthful to your soul; you may consider adding more of it into your life. Similarly, if you feel a large sense of fulfilment or peace when you help a neighbor mow their lawn or shovel their driveway, it's a sign that you should consider bringing more "givingness" into your daily experience.

On the other hand, if you feel jealous when you hear about a friend's healthy sex life or positive relationship with his or her spouse, it may be a sign that your own relationship is in need of assessment.

The following are just a few of the emotions that signal a Reinvention may — or may not — be in order. Look through the following list, and consider which emotions apply to you. This exercise could unearth some deeper emotions within you. It's OK to feel them! In fact, you won't ever find the life you wish to lead without doing so.

RE:INVENTION POWER TOOL

#12
ASSESS THE MESS —
MORE OR LESS?

For each of the emotions below, ask yourself two critical questions: "What makes me feel the emotion 'X'? and "How can I bring more or less of it into my life?"

Joy	Resentment/Bitterness
Fulfilment	Anger
Inspiration	Recklessness
Energetic	Guilt
Peace	Anxiety
Purpose/Accomplishment	Sadness/Depression
Gratitude	Frustration/Irritation
Jealousy	

Be still; listen to your inner voice, and, if you're not hearing it, allow yourself more time to search for the soul-provoking thoughts that are indicators of what you need and want. With all the noise, activity, people, obligations and responsibilities in our lives, sometimes we just have to sit back and *be* instead of *do*, and be kind enough to allow ourselves these moments. Everything else can wait . . . but you can't.

THE WILL TO LIVE DESPITE THE FEAR

Charlie's story is a compelling account of fear and Reinvention driven by a will to live and a passion that drove him to be one of the most inspirational individuals I've ever met.

From the lowest elevation on the planet — the depths of the Dead Sea — Charlie Engle is about to embark on one of the greatest adventures of his life. He will swim, free-dive, run, paddle, mountain bike and climb his way through multiple countries across wondrous and varied landscapes and complete his journey on the very tip of the earth — Mount Everest.

Talk about a Reinvention! This is far from where Charlie's story started . . .

Until Charlie was 29 years old, his life was consumed by an intense addiction to crack cocaine and alcohol. He faced some close calls, including a life-or-death moment that literally changed his life. It was then Charlie realized that no one had the power to save him other than himself.

"Someone shooting at me was absolutely an Ah-Ha Moment. Or maybe more like an *'Oh, Shit!'* moment!"

Drugs allowed him to escape from the realities of real life and his utter lack of self-confidence. His fear of dying as a hard-core drug addict motivated him to get sober. Then, the birth of his son gave him a whole new feeling of hope, but it was not quite enough at first, which led to his last binge.

"The odds were that I was going to die as an addict. It could happen in an instant, or, even worse, it could have taken years. But instead of accepting that result as certain, I chose a different path. I tried to quit a hundred times, but I just never could stick with it. Then my first son was born. I was sure that he could save me, that I would stay clean for him. A few months after his birth, I remember holding this perfect beautiful boy in my hands and feeling love that I never knew existed. As an addict,

I just thought I was broken, not deserving of love in any form. But holding him gave me hope and strength that I hadn't felt in years.

So it was with astonishment that I found myself driving to the worst part of town, where I spent six days smoking crack and destroying myself. That binge ended with me sitting on the ground, watching the police search my bullet-riddled car — bullets that had been intended for me. I watched a policeman pull a glass pipe from under the driver's seat and turn to look at me as he did. I should have been terrified about what might happen next, but all I could think was, 'So that's where that pipe was.' I was sick, and it was in that moment that I had the clearest thought . . . my son can't save me — nobody is coming to save me. Only I can choose between living and dying.

I used AA and my running community to help me through the good and bad times. There is huge power in mutually shared suffering, in going through hard things with others, helping them and letting them help me."

Charlie's fears pushed him both towards and away from his addiction. Before he was an addict, his worries revolved around feeling that he was not good enough. His strong urge to maintain perfection and please everyone around him were defining factors that led him to his addiction and relapses.

Charlie's passion for adventure, exploration and running kept him from falling through the cracks and relapsing, as he had many times before. After a long and hard journey to get clean, Charlie finished a total of 30 marathons within his first three years of sobriety. From there, he started pushing himself even further by entering races consisting of hundreds of miles all around the world, ranging from dense jungles to tall mountains to scorching deserts.

Ultimately, he became the first person to run 5,000 miles across the entire length of the Sahara Desert. In 2007, he partnered with Matt Damon to make a documentary film of the adventure. Together they started "H2O Africa," raising more than $6 million during the run. Today, the organization is known as WATER.org, the world's largest clean-water foundation. Now, he calls himself a "professional adventurer."

"These experiences taught me that I wanted to continue being a cultural explorer, an adventurer who travels on foot or on a bike, rather than by car or tour bus. I want to feel, touch, smell and fully immerse myself in the places and among the people around me. There is nothing to be gained from standing on the edge as an observer, at least not for me. I want to be all in, all the time."

His latest adventure — from the Dead Sea to the top of Mount Everest — will take him across every ecosystem on the planet. He calls this project "5.8," because, even though it's more than 4,200 miles from the bottom to the top of the planet, it's actually only 5.8 vertical miles between these ends of the Earth. "Everyone on Earth lives within this tiny 5.8 sliver of space. We are truly all in it together, and I want to show everyone the magnificent planet where we all live."

CHAPTER 7:
CYA
(AKA COVER YOUR ASS)

"Happiness is not something ready-made.
It comes from your own actions."

— Dalai Lama

Some of us see change coming from a distance, but many of us don't. Often, we are so set in our routine (even if it's not exactly what we want) that we don't plan for the road ahead. In anyone's life, there are distinct moments when it is necessary to contemplate what the next step might be.

PAY ATTENTION

There are quiet Ah-Ha Moments that we barely notice or we sweep under the rug, and then there are loud ones that cannot be ignored, drive us to change and disrupt our norm.

Here, we focus on listening to the voice in your head that speaks to you about impending change. It's the same voice referenced in Chapter 1, when I talked about the moment you realize you're in need of a Reinvention. Are you feeling the little poke that makes you question if you're in the right relationship or the right job? Are you spending your time the way you want? Do you feel a pull to be more socially active or a call to explore your spirituality more fully?

> *"To achieve great things, two things are needed:*
> *a plan and not quite enough time."*
> — Leonard Bernstein

When you know that a change is coming or feel the desire to create that transformation, that's when you need to *sit up and listen.* Pay attention to what's happening around you. Don't sweep reality under the rug as we're so inclined to do.

Is your company about to be acquired? Is that new consultant they brought in talking about downsizing? Have you noticed your spouse comes home later and later? Has your child become withdrawn and moody? Don't ignore the obvious signs all around you! You can get ahead of potentially huge life pitfalls — losing a job, marital trouble, emotional problems with your children — by paying attention to the signs that scream, "Change is afoot!" Instead of burying your head in the sand, which *seems* easier in the short term, start thinking about a plan of action.

My friend Daryn Kagan had the wherewithal to look at the road ahead in her career, and, in doing so, she got in front of a hard blow. For nine years, Daryn served as CNN's mid-morning news anchor of *Live Today.* She was also the host of the CNN/*People* magazine news/entertainment program *People in the News* and earlier served as a CNN sports reporter and anchor. Over the years, she built a loyal fan base of viewers.

At CNN, and all television networks, employment is secured by an annual contract. There was always a risk that Daryn's contract would not be renewed at the end of each year. That possibility rattled around in the back of her mind. It was bound to happen eventually. There was no grey area.

Daryn never thought she'd have to think about that next chapter. Would she continue to work at a prestigious network, surrounded by hard, negative and often depressing news stories, or would she use her journalistic skills and business savvy in a different way? It wasn't until she was shown the door that she had to consider her options.

Having spent time covering hard news and in the trenches of the Gulf War, she'd seen enough negativity. She wanted to create something that would affect and inspire the many followers she had acquired on air over the years. Since she was always clever enough to start saving money and put a "just in case" plan together to prepare for the day her contract was not renewed, she might have been more prepared to deal with that gut-wrenching "We're not renewing your contract" moment than most folks would be. It was a hard fall when "someday" came and CNN didn't renew, but not nearly as hard as it would have been if she had been unprepared. *Her intention was to create her own options.*

"It was only after getting the gift of being let go that I allowed myself the question, 'What do I really want to be doing?'" Having the savings gave her the opportunity to ask and answer the question and take the leap into starting her own company.

She had a vision, a small nest egg, and a team she knew she could call on when it was time to spring into action, which she did, quite quickly.

As they say, the rest is history. Today, she has a self-made media company, has written two books, inspires hundreds of thousands of readers, and is frequently interviewed on network television. Between her TED Talk and *CBS Morning News* segment, she's right where she wants to be.

BUILD YOUR OWN BRAND

Daryn's success was not by chance. She had a "Reinvention plan in her back pocket," a strategy my dear friend Lesley Jane Seymour advocates. She, too, is a fabulous example of a career journalist and editor who was able to pivot quickly.

Among many accomplishments, Lesley was Editor-in-Chief at *Redbook, Marie Claire* and *More* magazines for a combination of close to two decades.

Given the evolution of content in today's digital world, not to mention the downsizing, acquisitions and sexism that plagued the publishing industry during her tenure, Lesley became a master at dealing with change.

One thing she learned was that building her personal brand and connecting with her readers were paramount to lasting success in the industry. As soon as the men in the ivory tower announced *More* was shuttering, Lesley was bombarded by her readers and "fans" (yes, *fans*!). They begged her to resurrect a media platform that would keep the community of women connected. So, she did.

She kicked into action to create the Covey Club — an online media platform, community and digizine that brings women together around all the relevant conversations we're having in society today. Covey Club is the antithesis of the old "mean girl" mentality and one of the most incredible experiences that was born out of Lesley's corporate ride.

It might not have happened (or, at least, so quickly), if she hadn't laid the groundwork and built her personal brand. She did so by putting herself out there and listening to what her readers actually wanted and needed in their lives. She collected information and filled her tool chest with what she would need when the time came.

What Lesley has found on this journey is that there are hundreds of women going through a similar experience. She is poised to guide, advise

"

ALWAYS HAVE OPTIONS, AND THE
CHOICES WILL BE YOURS.

and share the warning signs and tools to avoid the challenges that may come with an "unintended Reinvention." Covey Club is a safe place to explore and discuss the nuances of the before-during-after phases at this juncture in one's life. Through online discussions, CC podcasts, and real Reinvention stories, more women are finding advice and solutions to move through this phase with grace and inspiration. They are getting the insight they need to truly find their best selves again.

"Personal branding is about managing your name — even if you don't own a business — in a world of misinformation, disinformation, and semi-permanent Google records. Going on a date? Chances are that your 'blind' date has Googled your name. Going to a job interview? Ditto."
— Tim Ferris

I've conducted workshops on personal branding, and it's surprising how few people understand the concept, let alone how to develop it for themselves. Most people aren't great at tooting their own horn and promoting themselves. But there are "graceful" ways to represent yourself from a point of view that reflects your interests and platforms. It starts with identifying your traits, strengths and skills. You just need to get comfortable packaging them as part of your identity — just as there are, most assuredly, things to avoid in this social media age. Lesley did it right, slowly amassing a fan base and always listening to their needs.

"Life isn't about finding yourself. It's about creating yourself."
— George Bernard Shaw

The career zone is a common place to be caught without a Reinvention plan, but the importance of being proactive in other areas of your life cannot be overstated. The point is, if you sense change is afoot, don't just sit around and wait for the inevitable. Take control of the situation, and get ahead of it instead of being run over by it.

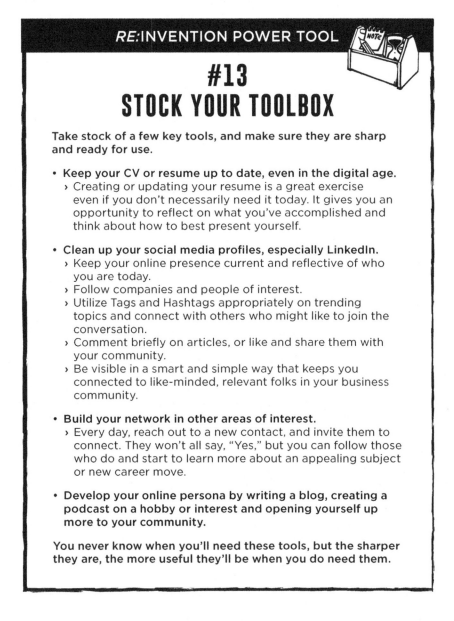

RE:INVENTION POWER TOOL

#13
STOCK YOUR TOOLBOX

Take stock of a few key tools, and make sure they are sharp and ready for use.

- **Keep your CV or resume up to date, even in the digital age.**
  - › Creating or updating your resume is a great exercise even if you don't necessarily need it today. It gives you an opportunity to reflect on what you've accomplished and think about how to best present yourself.

- **Clean up your social media profiles, especially LinkedIn.**
  - › Keep your online presence current and reflective of who you are today.
  - › Follow companies and people of interest.
  - › Utilize Tags and Hashtags appropriately on trending topics and connect with others who might like to join the conversation.
  - › Comment briefly on articles, or like and share them with your community.
  - › Be visible in a smart and simple way that keeps you connected to like-minded, relevant folks in your business community.

- **Build your network in other areas of interest.**
  - › Every day, reach out to a new contact, and invite them to connect. They won't all say, "Yes," but you can follow those who do and start to learn more about an appealing subject or new career move.

- **Develop your online persona by writing a blog, creating a podcast on a hobby or interest and opening yourself up more to your community.**

You never know when you'll need these tools, but the sharper they are, the more useful they'll be when you do need them.

When you know how to keep yourself focused on your goals and follow your "true north" or inner compass, all the right pieces will fall into place. I speak of a *plan* throughout this book, and, when we are mindful enough to create that plan, listen to ourselves, and allow ourselves to live our truth, we can't possibly be that surprised when it actually manifests and shows up in our life. We created it!

Whether you consciously develop the tools that move you from one place in your career or bounce from job to job in search of what inspires you, *be clear that there are no coincidences. You're being pulled by what interests you, so listen to it. This is the moment for you to realize that you ALWAYS have choices.*

Life doesn't show up on our front doorstep, as I found myself often telling my kids when they were younger. We must create our destiny and make plans to reach our dreams.

> *"Your beliefs become your thoughts,*
> *Your thoughts become your words,*
> *Your words become your actions,*
> *Your actions become your habits,*
> *Your habits become your values,*
> *Your values become your destiny."*
> — Mahatma Gandhi

CHAPTER 8:

HABITS: THE GOOD, THE BAD, AND THE UGLY

"We are what we repeatedly do. Success is not an action but a habit."
— Aristotle

A lot of us are so afraid of the unknown that we accept what we have instead of reaching for what might be. The saddest part is that we often assume our own failure. We assume that taking a risk will leave us poor, or broken or lonely. We have no faith that life could be better, richer and more fulfilling when we risk our current life to ask for more. Unhappiness becomes our favorite habit. After all, who could possibly be wealthy and successful doing what they actually love?

"Life supports all things based on their true nature."
— Alana Fairchild

It's understandable. The notion of a change, especially a sharp left, seems unfathomable. Our thoughts are entrenched. Our habits even more so. It feels impossible to change our kids' sports schedule, let alone our entire way of life.

"

FORGET "NEW YEAR'S"
RESOLUTIONS. MAKE NEW
OR "REINVENTED LIFE"
RESOLUTIONS — STARTING NOW.

*RE:*INVENTION POWER TOOL

#14
THREE TIMES
TO BECOME A HABIT

What's a passion that you'd love to rekindle? What's that one thing you keep saying you want to do or revisit? Was it learning a language? Playing the guitar? Painting? Photography? Cycling? Indulging in a hobby that makes you happy?

If you're having a hard time putting your finger on what it might be, try some of these exercises. Again — be still enough to listen and search inside yourself. What is the catalyst of those small Ah-Ha Moments?

Write your missing passion points down. Keep notes on:

• The things that make you smile in the course of your day

• The things that make your heart sing

• The thoughts that provoke curiosity and excitement

• The places you like to go

• The smells and sounds you like

• The dreams you have — sleeping or awake

These are all little signs of the things you want to surround yourself with in life.

Next, make a commitment to spend *three sessions* of time on one of those things. It doesn't matter how long the session is: it could be *three hours, three days or three evenings*. The point is to make a commitment to incorporate "it" into your life.

Once you make the commitment, you'll get "into it" and look for ways to calendar more sessions of time to indulge in an activity and create a habit.

Don't be discouraged if it's a multi-year plan. You have to start somewhere, so make that time *now*.

And yet it can be done.

But here's the rub: *Change can't happen in your life without . . . change.*

It means taking an honest look at our daily habits — mental and physical — and being willing to make a habit readjustment. It means being open to the good that is out there waiting for us, if only we'd let it in. That is what this chapter is all about.

Earlier, I shared that the number "three" was important to me, and, in a previous chapter, we focused on your three priorities. Now it's time to use the number "three" in a different way. You've probably heard the phrase: "If you do something three times, it becomes a habit." Let's use that fact to your advantage.

DIG DEEPER
(POWER TOOL #14)

- In the past, what personal habits have blocked you from experiencing your greatest good?

- How long have you struggled with those habits?

- How could those habits interfere as you reach toward your Reinvention goals?

- What can you do to re-wire your brain to make those issues less of a factor in your daily life?

We take for granted the daily habits that make up our routine. Often those habits are what block us. It's time to shake it up a bit. Have faith in who you'd like to be. Believe it's there. Go for it. Create it.

---

*RE:*INVENTION POWER TOOL

#15
CHANGE YOUR ROUTINE

Changing your routine is a good way to experience how invigorating different habits can be. Try simple things to start.

- Drive to a different coffee shop in your neighborhood
- Order an Iced Tea instead of an Iced Latte
- Wear the shoes in the back of your closet, rather than the ones you wear every day
- Try on a colored shirt instead of white with your suit
- Walk to the grocery store instead of driving
- Exercise in the morning vs. evening
- Read a book vs. watching a TV show
- Call an old friend for dinner
- Cook vs. ordering in
- Change your shampoo brand

Get the picture?

IF THEY CAN DO IT, I CAN DO IT

The more we see people succeed, break out of the norm, pursue their passions, make life happen, the more we realize we are not alone. They're not special; they don't have superpowers; they just dared to dream and went for it. It's time to start changing habits, dreaming bigger and believing you can do whatever you want to.

"

WANT TO BREAK OLD HABITS
AND CREATE NEW ONES? START
SMALL, AND GAIN CONFIDENCE
WITH THAT FEELING. YOU'LL FIND
THE JOY THAT COMES WITH
"MIXING IT UP" A LITTLE.

Reinventing your life comes in all shapes and sizes.

If you want to start working out, pick something fun, and start small. Take a beginner's class, and start slow, so that you're not in pain for a week and never want to go back.

You want to learn a language? Go on podcasts or the iTunes store, and download a language program — it's right there. Don't have time to do it? How about waking up 30 minutes earlier, taking a walk, and doing two great things at the same time every day? Can you imagine how you would feel after just 10 days?

My friend, Maureen tapped into one of her early passions, painting, when her life was in disarray. She had sketched and painted a little here and there throughout her life, but when she needed to reconnect with her true self, it was painting that allowed her to do so. The intensity of her life poured out in her re-found and reconnected talent. It became the center of her life and her joy. Today, patrons, friends and fans enjoy her artwork through exhibitions — something she never expected or intended.

She just started painting, so why can't you? You don't necessarily have to share or show your work to anyone, exhibit it or post it online. Do it for your own joy and to stretch your creativity.

> *"If you hear a voice within you say 'You cannot paint,' then by all means paint, and that voice will be silenced."*
> — Vincent Van Gogh

Do you believe others have skills greater than yours? Are they smarter? Do they have some special gene that makes them more capable than you? Or did they just summon the courage to try something they kept thinking and talking about?

If you actually spent one week changing your habits — not watching your favorite TV shows, not monitoring your social media — and you woke up 30 minutes earlier every day or cancelled lunch dates to try something you're interested in — writing, listening to language lessons, photography, planning a trip — you would be on your way. Just like that!

POSSIBILITY THINKING

Former client and now friend, fitness guru Kathy Smith, recently did a great interview on habits with a renowned doctor, Patrick Porter, MD, an award-winning author and founder of the Positive Changes Network. Through extensive research with "brain tap technology," Dr. Porter has helped people break the cycle of habits that are holding them back by changing the physiology of their bodies. He explains that physiology goes hand-in-hand with psychology, and we need to disrupt our body's patterns in order to break them.

Dr. Porter recommends utilizing a "Stop Sign Technique." When you find yourself in a negative thought pattern, simply say, "Stop," and think of three (there's that number again) alternate things you could do rather than think those thoughts. It could be anything: walk your dog, say an affirmation, read a book, go for a run — whatever it takes to re-map your brain from firing from its old, entrenched patterns.

Dr. Porter says, *"You get what you rehearse in life." You have to imagine what you want, or you will get what you've always gotten. Change your physiology; change your psychology.*

I know: if only it were always that easy! No matter how difficult it is, it is an important step to move toward a happier, more joyful, purposeful life.

One of the most difficult parts of "allowing" ourselves to Reinvent is that our "common sense" always tries to creep in. For that reason, it's important to remove your ego and "reasoning" mind from the picture. After all, Reinvention is not about the "*how*," it's about the "*why*" and the "*what*" — what you'd like to change to make your life a more fulfilling and enriching one.

> *"I had to realize that if my absolute best form of thinking resulted in me being in the state I was in (unhappy, miserable), then surely there was an error in the way I was thinking. I had to 'learn' a whole new way of seeing and being in the world."*
>
> — Bob Wosnitzer

In essence, we're talking about changing "probability thinking" to "possibility thinking." We need to stop thinking about what usually happens — what has happened in the past — and start thinking about what is possible. After all, this world is full of endless possibility. But so many of us seem to forget that!

> *"A pessimist sees the difficulty in every opportunity; an optimist sees the opportunity in every difficulty."*
>
> — Winston Churchill

PART 3:
EXCUSES, EXCUSES

CHAPTER 9:

THE DOG ATE MY HOMEWORK

"If you don't like the road you're walking,
start paving another one."
— Dolly Parton

Sometimes, when I'm talking to friends or colleagues, I get the sense that life is like a giant, never-ending, masochistic treadmill. We spend our days hammering away at work and then crawl back home for a hectic night of hitting the gym, paying the bills and getting the children to bed — only to wake up the next morning and start the drudgery all over again. *We do what we think we're SUPPOSED to be doing, rather than what we REALLY love.*

THE QUITTING CONUNDRUM

Many of us would rather stay the course, no matter how unhappy it is, than admit we want to change it. We feel like "quitting" our current path is a sign of failure, when it's really just the start — the foundation — for a happier life and the next adventure in our journey of life!

In a blog post, "Why Quitting Is Sometimes the Best Thing You Can Do," CreativeLive CEO Chase Jarvis shared how empowered he felt when he realized that quitting is a gift. "It wasn't that my job was too hard or that I wanted to give that up," he says. "It was that I realized I could live a much bigger, more meaningful life than I was currently living."

Chris is talking about far more than quitting a job. He's talking about the willingness to Reinvent *his own idea of success.* That is something that applies to all parts of our lives, from our jobs to our relationships to our legacies. *We need to realize the ride will never stop for us. We need to stop the ride.*

Just like the concept of "quitting," a new perspective can help debunk the excuses that may be holding us back from living a happier life. It's time to deconstruct our excuses. It's time to get this life moving again.

TAKE BACK YOUR LIFE

How about Gaye Dean's story? She decided to take a bold and courageous step toward Reinvention by asking her husband of 28 years for a divorce. They had been together since they were teenagers and had fallen into an unfulfilling routine.

Gaye is quick to say her marriage was not horrible. Her husband was both a kind man and a good father to their two boys. But he suffered from depression and experienced job instability. Gaye felt like she could never really be herself. Early in the marriage, she took the lead on most of the family decisions. She says, "It was like a snowball going down a mountain" as she took on more and more of the responsibilities by herself.

She accepts that she should have allowed for more of a partnership in the marriage, but once roles are assumed, it's easy for them to become the norm. There were other issues too, as is to be expected in any relationship of that length.

Mainly, Gaye worried. She worried about her husband, and she worried that she wasn't being true to her real self. She worried about blowing up her family and causing irreversible harm to the man she had been with all of her adult life, a man she cared for deeply.

From the outside, as is often the case, their lives looked great. Her friends thought she was happy with her beautiful home and job, her nice family and robust social life. It's not that Gaye didn't appreciate her life. She did, but she felt inauthentic within it.

Gaye knew in her heart she couldn't be married to her husband anymore. Their ideas and goals had changed, and they had drifted apart over the years. But she was still scared. She doubted herself. She worried she would regret her decision or wouldn't be able to live on her own. Would she be able to handle the stigma of being divorced? Could she find happiness as a middle-aged single woman?

"Being true to yourself is so important in finding your own happiness."
— Gaye Dean

It took two years for Gaye to work up the nerve to tell her husband (and best friend of 30 years) she wanted a divorce. He was stunned. After a lifetime of making decisions for the family, she made a very hard one for herself. She wasn't striving for perfection; she craved authenticity. Her mottoes then (and now) are: *"Take one day at a time, and care a little less,"* and *"By me not worrying so much what others think about me, I opened myself up to being able to be my authentic self."*

Gaye discovered she is a lot stronger and more resilient than she thought she was. Leaving her husband wasn't easy, but once she'd made the decision, she knew it was the right one. Best of all, none of her fears were realized. She and her ex-husband are on good terms, she is able to support her children, and she is enjoying life to the fullest. She was able to stop wondering what happened to her life and instead began to Reinvent it. She's in the midst of a fabulous career Reinvention now as well. And now she says, *"Only you can define you."* Gaye embodies one of her favorite quotes — *"Live the life you love, love the life you live."*

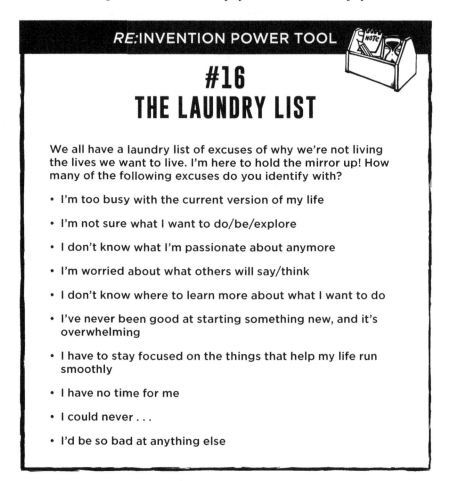

RE:INVENTION POWER TOOL

#16
THE LAUNDRY LIST

We all have a laundry list of excuses of why we're not living the lives we want to live. I'm here to hold the mirror up! How many of the following excuses do you identify with?

- I'm too busy with the current version of my life

- I'm not sure what I want to do/be/explore

- I don't know what I'm passionate about anymore

- I'm worried about what others will say/think

- I don't know where to learn more about what I want to do

- I've never been good at starting something new, and it's overwhelming

- I have to stay focused on the things that help my life run smoothly

- I have no time for me

- I could never . . .

- I'd be so bad at anything else

If you can relate to at least 2–3 of these excuses, it's time to take an even harder look at all the reasons why you *should* pursue a passion you've long yearned to pursue.

So, how are you going to do this? It won't happen all on its own. You have to consciously create your reality and your life to be what you want.

RE:INVENTION POWER TOOL

#17
DEBUNKING YOUR EXCUSES

This quick, stream-of-consciousness exercise asks you to draw three columns on a blank sheet of paper.

1. In the first, write what you'd like to add more of to your life.

2. In the second, write down your excuse for *not* doing so up until now.

3. And in the third, write a combination of both (e.g., "If I had more _____, I would _____.")

Now, get out your chisel! Are those excuses real? Take a moment to reflect on that now.

I'm serious. Put the book down, and really think about it.

WHAT I'D LIKE MORE OF IN MY LIFE.	MY EXCUSE FOR NOT DOING SO UP UNTIL NOW.	IF I HAD MORE _____, I WOULD _____ .

"

IT'S NOT LUCK; IT'S INTENTION,
A GOAL, A ROAD MAP AND A PLAN
TO GET THERE.

GOING FOR THE DREAM

Shannon Babcock was someone who was able to obliterate all of the excuses that stood in the way of what she wanted. She knew from a very young age that she wanted to have children. She was over the single life and tired of going out to bars all the time. She found that when she was out, she wished she had a family at home.

When she turned 39 and wasn't dating anyone seriously, she prepared to have a child on her own. She knew she could always get married later in life, but having a child would only get harder as she got older. A family member had advised her not to wait until everything in her life was "perfect" to have children, because that day would likely never come.

With the full emotional support of her parents, Shannon elected to use a donor to start her family. She had her first child just days before she turned 40. Before she gave birth, she learned that her donor was leaving the program, so she invested in the rest of the vials so she could give her new baby a sibling. Knowing she would be an older parent, she wanted her children to always have each other.

Shannon didn't get lost in excuses or self-doubt around her decisions. She was resolved. Although the fertility treatments gobbled up most of her savings, she knew she was investing in a future she had always dreamt about: being a mom and raising children. Getting pregnant a second time was not as easy as it had been the first, but she wasn't deterred.

She was afraid of how she would support her family on just one income and all by herself, without family in the area, but she didn't let the fear hold her back from her dream. Shannon says that now she worries about something happening to her, so she's making her own health and longevity a priority, even in the midst of raising two kids on her own.

Having children changed the entire trajectory of Shannon's life, most notably her career. Her job required a lot of time away from home, and the stress of trying to find childcare was too much. She started making decisions that were more family friendly than the corporate-ladder track she'd been on most of her life. She's embraced her new chapter with gratitude, determined to create a great life for her kids.

CHAPTER 10

THE ISSUE OF TIME

"Each and every moment of every day, we are always at a choice."
— Unknown

Ahhhh, time. That most precious gift.

There never seems to be enough of it. In fact, we all know that our time on this planet is limited. And yet, given how precious it is, you would think we would all spend it in the wisest ways possible, to create the life we truly wish to live. Not so, unfortunately!

MEETING THE RESISTANCE

There are two main questions that lead one to avoid, delay or resist Reinvention:

1. Are you truly willing to re-allocate your time to better support your dream?

2. Are you worried if it's the "right time" to make the changes you wish to see?

The good news is that we all have the power to determine both of those components — right now. But will we?

A business colleague, Brad Jakeman, is someone who admits to "thriving on ambiguity." He came to this realization after a dramatic decision. An important exercise led him to resign from a company and job he loved as President at PepsiCo, where he was working for a CEO who inspired him every day.

Brad's situation doesn't sound like he was ripe for Reinvention, but a good friend suggested he do a "Time and Motion" assessment of his work life. The exercise looks similar to the one I suggested in the previous chapter called "Debunking Your Excuses." The key difference is, in Brad's case, he was able to collect crucial data about how he spent his precious *time*.

Brad describes his experience this way:

> "Based on a friend's advice, I started to carry a notebook around at work. Each page of that notebook had three columns, in which I notated every task I did throughout the day for two solid months.

> The three columns were broken down according to the following criteria:

> 1. The things I loved to do: whatever inspired, motivated and/or challenged me.

> 2. The things I had to do but didn't particularly like doing.

> 3. The "conditions under which I was doing the things." Meaning, was I travelling, working from home, in a meeting, at the office, etc.

What I discovered over the course of two months was that my time was overwhelmingly filled with things I had to do versus things I loved to do. My time was spent on obligations as opposed to passions, and, worse, the conditions under which I was doing those things were far from ideal. Specifically, I realized I was travelling way more than I wanted to and not spending nearly enough time at the place I loved the most: my beach house."

Based on Brad's discoveries from the Time and Motion Survey, he made the decision to resign from his job. There was no turning back. Yes, he was scared about the loss of income and stability. However, the very next day, he felt more invigorated and enlivened than he had in years. Scarier than the loss of financial security was the fear that his life had become "too comfortable." Remember, Brad thrives on ambiguity, so the stability of a safe job was actually squelching his sprit.

Basically, he knew it was time to Reinvent. Whether it was the pull of a midlife crisis, a stirring from the "comfort" that was getting too familiar, the seductive lure of another yet-to-be-defined challenge, he just felt the tug, and it was time to go with it, no matter what the consequences. He was invigorated, excited and relieved despite the pit in his stomach.

Brad was also grappling with how deeply his sense of identity had been tied to his title and company. This is something I've heard over and over again from many of the people interviewed for this book and in other conversations. A role or a title can provide such a strong sense of identity that the individual gets lost in it or hides behind it. They stopped looking at *who* they were and focused on *what* they were. This is a common occurrence.

When Brad embarked on his Reinvention process, he started to recognize who his true friends were, not just those who "needed" him because of his role and access to business. He had to learn to stand tall as his own person and not the president of a massive company. Who returned his calls and emails now? Was he still invited to important industry events, or to speak on panels with fellow C-Suite executives?

Brad confessed, "My fear was that my value was inextricably tied to my career and specifically my job title. The fear that I may never do anything as big as what I was already doing. The fear that my job provided a platform, and that platform was the main thing, driving my own relevance." Interestingly, when he stepped out of his old role at PepsiCo, the offers, conversations and ideas for new opportunities started opening up to him in unimaginable ways. He created the space for something new, and, thus, his fears are allayed every day by the exciting options that are showing up in his life.

TIME DEBTING

On the other side of the coin, my friend Linda Sivertsen — *New York Times* bestselling co-author, book whisperer, agent, connector, seasoned midwife of bestselling books and six- and seven-figure book deals, creator of The Boyfriend Log app, and host of the Beautiful Writers Podcast — devised a fascinating method to examine the way she spent her time. It came to her when she was feeling overwhelmed by a toxic relationship. Similar to Brad's approach, hers is rooted in the idea of data collection.

Linda's process was to color code her online diary so she could easily identify the energy-sucking activities or appointments in her life. Color coding led Linda to some pretty profound realizations about what she was doing with her time.

"

**NO EXCUSES!
BE SHARP(E), BE CLEAR,
BE CONSCIOUS, BE ALIVE.**

In a TEDWomen Talk from 2016, Linda shares the events that led to one of her friends accusing her of being a "time debtor." She was given the label at 10 p.m. one night. She had just made a pot of black tea to caffeinate for yet another work-related all-nighter. Her friend Jade "wasn't having it." Jade had noticed some unhealthy patterns in Linda's life, and she made the bold move to call her out on them.

Linda hadn't heard the term "time debtor" before, but it immediately rang true. Time debting is the practice of spending your time incorrectly, borrowing against precious down-time hours to catch up with work. Was she wasting time she didn't have? She thought back to the 60 all-nighters she'd already clocked in that year alone to "keep from losing everything." She rationalized that, if she could just log more billable hours, she would be able to keep it together. As Linda says now, "Never mind that what I needed was more *life hours*."

Instead of managing her time, Linda's time was managing her. In her words, those all-nighters were zapping the quality of her all-dayers. What she thought was a net/net was in fact, a net/not.

Linda's talk resonated with many people in the realization that time debting is often a symptom of something deep (and dangerous). Some people spend all of their time at work because they're afraid they're not good enough. Others run themselves ragged so they don't have to feel (or deal) with their emotions. This last "why" was Linda.

She was able to see that the way out of this mess was to start tracking her time, in the same way she tracked her finances. Many people track time on their smartphone through various apps, but Linda took the concept a step further. She had to uncover the emotions beneath the surface so that she could get to the heart of "why." To do so, she started to color code the way she spent her time with how she felt during that time. Blue for sad, yellow for mellow, and green for romantic. She quickly discovered the colors don't lie. At a glance, it was easy to see most of her time was spent dealing with dysfunctional-relationship drama.

> *"Time is energy. It's our lifeblood.*
> *When we drain it away, it's gone."*
>
> — Linda Sivertsen

When Linda understood she was a time debtor and took the steps to better manage her time and her feelings, she was able to identify which emotions were robbing her of her lifeblood and her vitality. Her advice today: "Give yourself the gift of the time it takes to accomplish whatever matters most to you. Refuse to write a bad check on your greatest asset: your time, your life."

THE "RIGHT" TIME

Now for the big question: How do I know when it's the right time?

The inspirational gurus among us will tell you that the time is always now. In many ways, that is true. As demonstrated in the past few exercises, there are a multitude of things that you can start doing *today* to make your ideal life less of a dream and more of a reality. But what about the bigger things?

Yes, the time is always right for making positive changes. But the time is not always right to quit your paycheck or create any other version of mass chaos in your life.

In Brad Jakeman's case, he says the moment he decided to resign from his job is almost impossible to articulate. He just knew. If only we were all so lucky!

For most of us, it's a nagging sensation that something just isn't the right fit. Two years ago, my son went off to college to study medicine.

Ever since he was a young boy, he wanted to be a doctor. What mom wouldn't be thrilled? But after his first year, he came home incredibly unhappy. He wasn't inspired. He wasn't himself. Truth be told, there were way more math classes than he had foreseen.

At that moment, he knew he had a choice to make. Either struggle through and pursue a career he no longer wanted — or admit that his dream had changed. For my son, changing his major before he was too deep into core classwork was a smart decision. And he had both of his parents supporting him. It was the right time to speak up about a nagging feeling.

How many times have you been in that same situation? *What did you do about it?*

One of my favorite quotes is: *"The right thing at the wrong time is the wrong thing."* (Joshua Harris, *I Kissed Dating Goodbye*.) While I'm not a huge fan of the terms "right" and "wrong" when it comes to one's personal journey, I do believe that good, old-fashioned common sense can aid in creating a smoother and more joyful Reinvention experience.

CHAPTER 11

IF IT WASN'T FOR $, I'D _____

"My goal wasn't to make a ton of money. It was to build good computers."
— Steve Wozniak

The second biggest excuse people use when considering a major change in their life (right after time) is money. The excuses I hear most frequently from friends include:

"I can't afford . . ."

- that trip

- to take time off work

- to lose that client

- to make more time for myself

- a career change — especially at my age

"

IF MONEY WERE NO OBJECT,
WHAT WOULD YOU BE DOING
WITH YOUR LIFE?
YOUR ANSWER IS A GOOD MEASURE
OF WHERE YOU ARE NOW — AND
WHERE YOU WANT TO BE.

They say, "Kathi, I love your Reinvention talk, but fulfilment doesn't pay the bills!"

We, as human beings, are engineered to think this way. We live from a "lack mentality," perpetually believing that if we use what money we have, we will never be able to make more (contrary to years or decades of seeing the contrary). *We are our own biggest obstacles to better, more joyous, more satisfying lives.*

AFFORDING THE LIFE YOU WANT

One of the most important things you can do to determine the right timing for your Reinvention is to have an honest talk about your budget.

- How much do you need to live?

- How much can you put away toward your goal?

- Are you being honest about your financial situation?

Don't think only about your short-term needs. Think long-term. Big picture. How long would it take to get that new boat, to visit Italy, or to take a six-month sabbatical? In my experience, you may be surprised how doable a Reinvention can be.

DIG DEEPER

- How much do you need to live?

- How important is money to you in your ideal life?

- Will you be able to meet your current standard of living if you pursue your dream? Why or why not?

- What are you willing to do without to make your dream come true?

- What are you *not* willing to do without to make your dream come true?

- Where can you cut your budget to make room for your Reinvention goal? (Cheaper apartment or car, eat in, less shopping, etc.)

These are not easy questions. In fact, money can often be quite an emotional issue. It is possible you may not have the answers right away.

When my friend Bob (introduced in Chapter One) left his six-figure job on Wall Street to pursue a degree in media studies, he took a severe pay cut — dropping to just $30,000 a year. While the decision meant a dramatic lifestyle change, including moving from trendy Tribeca to working-class Queens, Bob says it also gave him the chance to get rid of a lot of material things and redefine his own idea of success and happiness.

That's not to say it was easy. Bob's journey was riddled with bumps in the road and serious moments of doubt and fear, largely due to mounting student debt and his lower salary. At one point, he nearly left his Master's program to return to Wall Street, until friends and mentors offered to help him finance the remainder of his coursework because they knew how much it meant to him.

"Chances are good that you will have a slight 'relapse' or begin to lose faith once you set your Reinvention in process," Bob shares. "With

*RE:*INVENTION POWER TOOL

#18
THE BUDGET

If you don't already have one, take a moment to create a budget of your life.

Hard Expenses

Mortgage/Rent	Food, groceries
Internet/Cable/Phone	Health Insurance
Car Payment	Taxes
Car Insurance	Clothes
Credit Card Payments	Childcare
Student Loans	Caretaking (parents)
Gas	Tuition

Soft Expenses

Entertainment	Restaurants
Travel/Holidays	Gifts
Kids' Activities	Savings
Concerts	Total Expenses
Retirement	Income vs. Expenses (+/-)

matters of money and self-doubt, it's possible to lose sight of the reasons you embarked on your Reinvention journey in the first place. *The trick is to re-set your attitude every day, to approach each challenge with the same intention and enthusiasm you felt when you first decided to make a change, and, of course, to trust your path and be open to everything it brings you."*

*"I had decided to stop chasing the money
and start chasing the passion."*

— Tony Hsieh

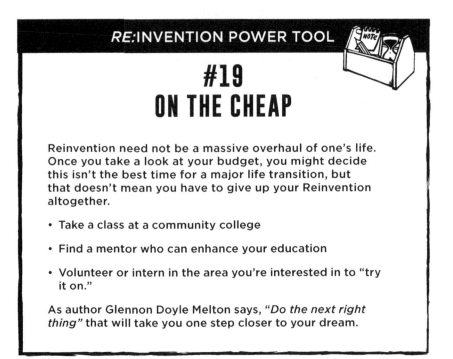

RE:INVENTION POWER TOOL

#19
ON THE CHEAP

Reinvention need not be a massive overhaul of one's life. Once you take a look at your budget, you might decide this isn't the best time for a major life transition, but that doesn't mean you have to give up your Reinvention altogether.

- Take a class at a community college

- Find a mentor who can enhance your education

- Volunteer or intern in the area you're interested in to "try it on."

As author Glennon Doyle Melton says, *"Do the next right thing"* that will take you one step closer to your dream.

"Man sacrifices his health in order to make money. Then he sacrifices money to recuperate his health. And then he is so anxious about the future that he does not enjoy the present moment. As a result, he does not live in the present or the future; he lives as if he is never going to die, and then he dies having never truly lived."

— The Dalai Lama

There is always something you can do to be happier. Take a look at the examples on the next page, and consider whether there are ways to incorporate more of your dreams into your daily life.

Goal	Budget Option
Get a degree in counseling	Volunteer at a crisis center
Visit Italy	Take an Italian-language course
Buy a new motorcycle	Join a club/rent one
Pursue a career in music	Join a band and play locally

Sometimes it's better to take the budget route than jump in with both feet! After volunteering at the local crisis center, you may realize you don't enjoy counselling as much as you thought you would, or you might find another passion altogether. Either way, it never hurts to try. Test the waters. Try different things to figure out what connects for you. *The Reinvention evolution is always upward.*

> *"For me, the opposite of scarcity is not abundance. It's enough. I'm enough."*
> — Brene Brown

Chris Pepe decided to take a leap, on a restricted budget, to pursue something he and his family were passionate about: the notion of "leaving it all behind." Even if only for a year, they wanted to explore their roots and life in another country and escape Silicon Valley for a year in Italy.

Chris left his full-time, corporate job — one that many would clamor for — his wife also left her job, they pulled their kids out of school, and they moved to Italy. The Pepes didn't necessarily have the financial means to approach the adventure from an extravagant angle, but because they really wanted to make it happen, they were calculated and clever in their approach.

They rented out their house to contribute to the rent on a place in Italy. They researched suitable schools for the kids in an area where they had relatives. They had a destination they'd visited before and a mission in mind. What would happen once they arrived was anyone's guess, but they were game for the adventure.

The Pepes' year in Italy was an unparalleled opportunity for the family to unplug, connect with their roots, with each other, with the culture and with life on a level none of them had ever experienced. They nurtured their souls and their minds living in a foreign land, exploring the areas around them, going to school, digging into new hobbies and passions, and living in a way that many of us only ever dream of.

It was a slice in time when they dared to dream, and they explored, as we all deserve to in this one, big, beautiful life. They made ends meet; they reprioritized what they needed to thrive. Their definition of happiness and success completely shifted. A collective accumulation of experiences, not possessions, became the priority, and living life was always at the center.

The hardest aspect of the trip was coming home and recalibrating to what felt like an easy and "regular" life. Going back to their old schools, regular jobs, and the supermarket wasn't quite the same after the sights, colors, tastes and sounds of the magnificent Northern Italian way of life.

But there is still a skip in Chris's step and a glimmer in his eye. Knowing he really "did it" and could do it again — that he had the courage to make it work — is an extraordinary life lesson for Chris, his wife and their kids. The gift he has given his kids is life-changing — one that features a multi-cultural and bilingual life, and an appreciation for the bounty that exists in their Silicon Valley life.

Reinvention does not have to be a financial goal or challenge. It can be powered by a dream and the sheer will to achieve it. How you get there — whether it's trading houses, saving money for 10 years, volunteering, taking up a hobby in your spare time — doesn't entirely matter. What matters is figuring out how to fulfill your dreams and achieve the Reinvented Life you aspire to.

PART 4:
REALITY CHECK

CHAPTER 12

LIFE MATTERS

*"In the long run, we shape our lives, and we shape our-
selves. The process never ends until we die. And the choices
we make are ultimately our own responsibility."*

— Eleanor Roosevelt

Hey, we're not all young, rich and single. Most of us are none of those things! If you have children or a high-profile job, it can be difficult (if not impossible) to give up a great income for the uncertainty of a new, more-fulfilling life. If you're in between and trying to find your "thing," you may not have the luxury or money to support this decision.

BACKYARD REINVENTIONS

That doesn't mean you can't make plans to Reinvent right at home. Valerie Lewis did just that when she was raising her family. She started a photography business, Pic in the Park, when she was searching for a cool way to connect with her three sons. Taking pictures at their sporting events got her up off the bleachers and onto the sidelines, where her kids enthusiastically recounted what she had just captured at games or matches.

Valerie wasn't a formally trained photographer. She taught herself by reading books and practicing. Eventually, she got to the skill level where she invested in a good lens. Soon, her approach to spending more time with her kids evolved into a business. Her sons' friends wanted senior portraits at an affordable price, so they went to her. Next thing she knew, she had a full-blown business shooting weddings, executive portraits and more.

When her kids were in high school, Valerie reinvented again, and again, it was due to them. She was frustrated by the lack of direction around all of the choices for the college years. There was almost no information available for students who weren't quite ready for college or who would benefit from going in a different direction.

All three of Valerie's kids chose to go abroad by themselves for one reason or another, and she saw the benefits of youth volunteer work and independent travel. She started a service called College Bound Now in response to the need for better information about alternatives to the traditional route.

Again, Valerie's new venture was self-taught. She researched and read up on the almost-endless list of opportunities. Her target audience was camped out in her own living room after school every day, watching her TV and eating her snacks.

She dove in by helping her kids' friends with their college essays and selection lists. Word started to get around, and soon Valerie was hosting free workshops to help kids and parents navigate the process.

College Bound Now grew into an all-inclusive business that provides guidance for the entire selection process, testing advice, scholarships, gap years — everything she had needed help with when her kids were trying to figure it all out.

Eventually, Valerie grew her business into an affordable membership site with short tutorials. Her intention is to make it available to as many people as possible.

*RE:*INVENTION POWER TOOL

#20
ASSESS YOUR
RESPONSIBILITIES

- Take an honest look at your current responsibilities.

- Which ones can you outsource to someone else to allow greater time and flexibility in your life?

- Of those you can't (raising children, caring for aging parents), how can you incorporate them into your Reinvention goals or pace your Reinvention to align with their needs?

- What are your "need to do's"? Make your list as detailed as you like, from dropping off/picking up kids at school (which creates a hard start/stop to your day) to financially supporting your family or parents.

It might look something like this:

People	Activities	My To-Do
Abigail	Ballet (M & W)	Coordinate pick-up with Nancy's mom
Fido	Flea bath	Call vet for appointment
Sammy	Baseball practice	Team snack
Trish	Walmart Deck	Research consumer stats
Jo	Parents	Visit & Spend Time/Doctor Visit/Bills

What responsibilities stand in the direct path of the life you wish to live? For instance, "My full-time job makes it difficult to spend time writing a new book," or "I spent 20 hours a week caring for my dad, and that makes it difficult to focus on my own needs or desires."

She also started a company that explores international volunteer opportunities as a means to get out and give back on a global level called "Gel'n," which is an acronym for her personal philosophy: *Give, Explore, Love Now. It's a pursuit that feeds her love of travel and her natural tendency to care for others.* She is linking Gel'n with College Bound Now by adding a donation aspect to groups that build schools abroad — thus tying her two passions together.

Despite the responsibilities that come with being a mom and running a household, Valerie knew she needed something for herself. She found creative opportunities to blend her role as a parent with her entrepreneurial spirit. All right in her own backyard. Through service to others, Valerie is continually Reinventing, using her responsibilities and life practicalities as fuel.

> *"It is not a daily increase, but a daily decrease.*
> *Hack away at the inessentials."*
> — Bruce Lee

Dr. Gail Matthews, a psychologist and professor at the Dominican University in California, studies the art and science of goal setting. She discovered that *people who write their goals down are 42% more likely to achieve them than those who don't.* Who wouldn't want to be in that statistic? Try it!

Here are my big "life" wishes:

- More time with my family

- A chance to follow the passions and hobbies I've neglected lately

- The ability to be more productive without feeling like a "Type A" personality

- Plant an herb-and-vegetable garden in our backyard. (I've been thinking about this one for a while.)

- Travel internationally on a regular basis and discover things I've never seen or done.

Most of us don't stop long enough to make a "Big" Life Wish List, let alone execute on it. Put it out there, and make it happen.

RE:INVENTION POWER TOOL

#21
YOUR "BIG" LIFE WISH LIST

Take out a fresh piece of paper (and don't roll your eyes!) and really think about the things you want in your life. Not the materialistic things — the big "life" things. For example:

- Travel more
- Volunteer
- Learn a language
- Relocate
- New Job

- Write a book
- Exercise four times a week
- Create a more expansive social and cultural life
- Find time to do nothing and just be still

Most people say, "Yeah, yeah. I know what I want. I have the list in my head, and it just isn't coming together." That's because you have to write it down. Force the moment, and create intention and goals in your life.

"

**STOP DREAMING
AND START DOING.**

RE:INVENTION POWER TOOL

#22
AN ACTION PLAN FOR DOING INSTEAD OF DREAMING

Once you've made your wish list for the future, take it a step further. Here are several action items you can take today to move closer towards your "Big" Life Wish List and desired future outcome:

- Identify *why* you want to Reinvent this part of your life (more excitement, a richer education, more money).
  › Is it something you've always dreamed of?
  › Will it make you happier?
  › Will it make someone else in your life happier?
  Knowing why you're embarking on a Reinvention will always bring you back to the core when challenges arise.

- Identify what you want to achieve and when you will start. Do it with true intention.

- Share what you're doing with others.
  › You'll be surprised how many people in your inner circle know someone or something that could be helpful to you. Plus, they'll encourage you on your path.
  › Also, when we share something, we feel more accountable.

- Establish the challenges you anticipate, and come up with a plan to overcome these obstacles — create a "no excuses" situation for yourself, and don't become a victim of your own circumstances.
  › It may be time, it may be money, it may be lack of knowledge, it may be fear.
  › Whatever it is, knowing that there will be challenges and creating the mindset that you'll meet them head-on and stick to your plan is super productive.

- Create a mini-reward system for yourself.
  › When you achieve a milestone, no matter how small, do something to acknowledge and reward yourself.
  › Pat yourself on the back, share with a friend, tally it in a journal, have an ice cream, watch that TV show you recorded — whatever gives you that sense of pride and acknowledgement, allow yourself that indulgence and positive reinforcement.

AN UNEXPECTED REINVENTION

When something reminds you of how precious your life is, you really start to re-think what you'd do if you were confronted with that question way before you were ready to deal with it. Stephanie's story exemplifies an unexpected Reinvention.

Stephanie worked in politics with Senator Joe Biden, then the entertainment industry with Cartoon Network/Turner Broadcasting/Hanna-Barbera Cartoons, and then on to President of Global Consumer Products, Gaming Partnerships and Product Placement for Universal Pictures. She launched famed multi-billion dollar programs and franchises, before she was appointed president of the Imagine Entertainment's Kids & Family division, all while continuing the current CEO role of her own company White Space Entertainment.

And when you hear Stephanie's story, it makes you realize what love, hope and a great attitude can do to keep you going, Reinvent your life and live out your dreams on your own terms . . . even when the doctor has just handed you a "so-called death sentence."

A little more than 10 years ago, 9/11 took on a new significance for Stephanie. It was on that date, years later, that she was diagnosed with breast cancer.

I'm sharing a *Redbook* excerpt from an interview with Stephanie as she tells her story with such grace and inspiration:

On the morning of September 11, 2007, my heart was bursting. I was the mother of a chatty five-year-old ecstatic about her first week in kindergarten, and I was working as a studio executive in Hollywood, strategizing million-dollar licensing deals. I was on the top of my game. At 42, I felt like life was finally restarting on my own terms. After a brutal divorce, I felt sexy and giddy in love: I was in the magical first months of a heart-shaking, palm-sweating romance with a sexy independent film producer I met at work.

We had flirted over emails for a month, and when we finally met for a scotch, we made out like teenagers in an alley outside. As I got ready to head out of my house to the office, I saw my doctor's number on the caller ID. I didn't feel nervous as I picked up. I had gone the week before to check on the tiniest pebble of a bump in my nipple, something I wondered about even worrying about. It was nothing like the fibroids I'd had in my breasts years earlier.

Then the doctor's words sent waves of shock through my body. "We've found something," she said. "You're going to have to come in."

Holy shit, I thought.

"It's cancer. I'm sure it's not the bad kind," she said. "But come on into the office, and we'll go over the report when it comes back."

By 3 p.m., I was sitting in a chair, clutching the hands of a friend who had come with me, as my surgeon told me they had detected triple negative cancer, the most aggressive kind, in my breasts — and it had already spread to one lymph node. The test also showed I was BRCA-positive, which meant that, after six months of chemotherapy, a double mastectomy and 36 sessions of radiation, I would need to have both of my ovaries removed. If I survived, I would go into an instant and very early menopause. The treatment would have to begin immediately if I was to have any chance.

Cancer patients will tell you that there's a brief, strange moment in their life *between* "*before*" — when you're healthy, walking the streets running errands and living life, and "*after*," when you find out you're not. That was definitely true for me. Suddenly, I felt like I didn't belong to the regular world. I knew I might die, and I felt totally alone, even though the room was packed with friends and doctors explaining how they were going to be there for me. My body shaking, I headed out to my car after the visit was over. I tried to reassure my friend that I was okay, but I had to be alone. I had to get into my car and talk to Andy. *Cancer — what the fuck are you talking about?* I thought as my trembling fingers hit the numbers. *I have a five-year-old. I'm in love.*

I tried to calm my tone as I told him the news. But instead, it all came out in a flow of choked words.

"If you want to get out of this, I won't think you're a jerk," I said. "We were having a blast. You don't have to take care of me. You don't have to see me through this ugly process." First, there was silence. Then, he started laughing. "I'm not going anywhere. We're going to get through this together — this is temporary."

I was afraid of losing my hair. I dreaded it, and I dreaded the whole process. As I started to get the treatments, with my friends always at my side, I felt trapped — imprisoned. There was no way out. The treatment was an intense cocktail. In the first course of chemo, there was even a skull and crossbones on every bag they pumped into my body; it was crazy poisonous, and it made me feel like I wanted to crawl out of my skin — like how they show heroin addicts going through withdrawal in the movies.

Nineteen days into treatment, my hair started really falling out, as predicted. I cried one afternoon, looking at the long strands covering the floor. I called Andy, and he came right away. He sat me in a chair on my patio with a glass of wine and a pair of shears. First, he cut off my blonde ponytail. Then he shaved my head. Tentatively, with a few sips of that wine in me, we walked together to the bathroom mirror. I hid behind him. I didn't want to see myself bald — mostly because of what it represented. But he stepped to the side, and we looked at the image staring back together. "Actually," he said, as a similar shock of recognition pulsed through my body, "it's kind of sexy." *When I looked, really looked, I realized it didn't look that bad. I was sexy. My hair and my breasts were not things I needed to feel like a woman. In that moment, it was the intimacy and the deep connection we had to each other.*

I worked through the whole process. I wore a white bandana and giant hoop earrings. It's hard to put on eyelashes every day, but I did it. We went to go see plays and have dinner. People would look at me and be uncomfortable, but I was okay with it. My skin yellowed, and I had bad breath.

But I pushed through it every single day. Andy and I treated it like a temporary condition. A year of hell. Chemo, a double mastectomy. Reconstruction. Radiation. My ovaries removed. Menopause at 42. Why would I want them around? As a younger woman, I had always the feeling that maybe that sense of strength and confidence was actually false . . . like I could be faking it. Going through this made it clear that I'm tougher than I ever knew — no faking! Viking tough. Stuff at work, stuff at school — nothing scared me like it used to. Or got to me.

A year after I finished the treatment, we decided to move in together. When we spoke about it, he said, "I love you. I don't want to be with anyone else; I just don't want to get married." I didn't care if we were married or not. I trusted his commitment, and I felt like we could just be boyfriend and girlfriend until we were 90. But then, about two years into living with one another, on a visit to New York City together after a romantic dinner, he pulled me into an alley and got on one knee. He asked me to marry him. Of course, I said "Yes" immediately. We've been together for 12 years, and Andy's a wonderful father to my daughter, and life is great.

It's been a little more than ten years for me, and I'm still here. I do regular checkups and blood work. I'm great. I know what's scary and what's not. Now, more than ever, I know how to live.

Stephanie's Reinvention might have been forced on her, but her spirit and fortitude are a huge reminder to all of us that *it is our choice to frame our circumstances and create the best out of it*, no matter what the challenges. No one can walk in our shoes, but to see the way this hard-working, loving woman chose to charge through treatments, her job, and embrace her love for her daughter, her (now) husband and friends as her support system, is a testament to Stephanie and all that we can learn from her.

NEVER GIVE UP

Make a true commitment to searching for better and demanding more for yourself. And never stop. It's my view that there should be no cap to our vision of happiness and wonderment. Appreciate where you are in the present, and seek more every single day.

An example of someone who never stops striving to be better and do more is my friend Diana Nyad. Diana is an American author, journalist, motivational speaker and long-distance swimmer. She gained national attention in 1975, when she swam around Manhattan and again in 1979, when she swam from North Bimini, The Bahamas, to Juno Beach, Florida.

On September 2, 2013, on her fifth attempt and at the age of 64, Diana became the first person to swim from Cuba to Florida — 110.86 miles in 52 hours, 54 minutes, and 18 seconds — without a shark cage! I've had the privilege of working with her through my marketing agency and helped Diana and her expedition partner and best friend, Bonnie Stoll, with the launch of their new movement, EverWalk™.

At 66 years old, not ready to rest on her laurels, Diana and Bonnie started this exciting venture called EverWalk™, which strives to get people across America up and moving. To promote their idea, they created a series of walking events, a website, a community of global walkers and a series of EPIC EverWalk events — each one consists of seven days of walking from one amazing city to the next.

At the time of this writing, along with hundreds of enthusiastic walkers seeking "their EPIC," they've walked from Los Angeles to San Diego, Boston to Cape Elizabeth, Maine, Vancouver to Seattle, and Philadelphia to Washington, DC.

From the moment I met Diana, I was riveted by her story, her laser-focused determination and her unwavering quest for what's possible. Diana embodies the spirit of "Never Give Up." Her legendary career is rooted in her incredible sense of drive and passion and a formidable spirit that always inspires those in her midst. With her support, I participated in the first-ever EPIC EverWalk event between Los Angeles and San Diego, and completed my own personal first — an EPIC 33 miles.

Diana is a constant reminder in my life that you can do *anything* you set your mind to and work hard for. She drives me to strive harder at everything I do — and I thought I'd already been doing that my whole life!

"Whenever you're pushing through the tough moments, find a way. If something is important to you, and it looks impossible, and you're up against it, step back for a minute, and ask yourself if you have the resolve to think of every -nth degree to get through this. And most times, we do."

— Diana Nyad

CHAPTER 13:

WHAT (OR WHO) IS HOLDING YOU BACK?

"You were born with wings; why prefer to crawl through life?"

— Rumi

Do you find yourself living vicariously through others — marveling over their Instagram pages (feeling envious), reading stories of amazing adventures that others dared to take on, or hearing about complete 360-degree life changes?

Then it's time to do something about it.

COMPLACENCY VERSUS CREATIVITY

Some of us stumble upon things in our lives and transition from one thing to the next — jobs, relationships and health issues. Others create those changes, consciously, deliberately and with intent — there's fear, there's trepidation, there's a sense of adventure.

Which category do you fall into? Do you wish and wait and watch others pass you by, *or* do you take charge of your life and create what you want? Do you wish you could take a bold step and create something new, break out of your comfort zone and be "one of them"?

What's holding you back? Is it someone? Are you surrounded with people who tell you it would be ridiculous to try to lose that much weight, or switch careers, or pursue a talent, or save money for that trip you've always dreamed of? Is anyone in your life saying, "You could never do that!"

At some point, we have to realize we can pursue the things we want and overcome those naysayers and "show them!"

I think many of us would envy Marla Baldassare, my longest, closest, best friend since high school. In our adult lives, we got to see each other every month, since she moved to New York for a job, and I visited the city every month to meet with agency clients. I probably saw Marla more often than I saw my friends in LA! But when Marla told me that, after 20 years of being the quintessential New Yorker, she was uprooting her family from their beautiful newly renovated brownstone in trendy Harlem and moving to a seaside village in New Hampshire — with a population smaller than what would fit in the LA Staples Center — I was shocked.

Marla and her family decided it was time for a lifestyle Reinvention! They took their kids out of their high schools, sold their lakeside vacation home and up and moved to a beautiful town they'd visited. They loved and dreamed of what life could be like . . . and just did it. Yes, literally, just like that!

Her husband could run his business from home and commute to headquarters on a regular basis across the country. She would find a new job doing something completely different, and she did. Thus, they started their enviable life in a beautiful town with lovely people who aren't stressed 24/7 from trying to keep up with the rat race. They are enjoying a quality of life that most people only dream about.

Taking it a step further, Marla is now living out the courageous life of an entrepreneur, coupling her personal passion for social impact and the sustainability of our planet with her business savvy. She's launched a retail store called WE FILL GOOD to help eliminate plastic waste. Customers can refill their own containers with eco-friendly products, such as hand soap, dish soap, laundry detergent, shampoo and body lotion. They can also choose household and personal-hygiene products that are plastic-free, such as bamboo toothbrushes, produce bags, stainless steel to-go containers and bandages.

Many of us wouldn't dare to make such a move, but, with a little planning and a lot of gumption, Marla and her family are living a Reinvented life and have found a new way to appreciate all that they have.

"Our lives improve only when we take chances — and the first and most difficult risk we can take is to be honest with ourselves."

— Walter Anderson

Reinventing has been in my bones every day of my life — shifting and moving with the highs and lows of business, figuring out how to prioritize my children and family life and creating down-time with a tenacious work and travel schedule. I've been an entrepreneur my whole life. I started at 24 years old and never looked back.

As a young woman, facing a "man's world" and the heaping challenges that could have thrown me into the arms of corporate America, security and a steady paycheck, how many times do you think I was told "It can't be done," "You'll never get that business," "Why don't you just get something steady?"

Now what fun would that have been? Not only have I created what I love to do and worked with companies and clients I thoroughly enjoy, but I've been my own boss since I started working. The creativity and business acumen to control my own destiny have been the greatest gifts I could have given myself. I have landed on the right balance and feel energized by both, cultivating my creative side with hobbies and interests that fulfill me. It's in my DNA to lean in — it's all I know. And that's just what I kept doing!

If you can't put yourself and your inner voice first, you'll never be able to forge the path to get where you're trying to go. With that inner strength, certainty and courage, it will be a lot easier to face those who say, "You can't possibly be considering that career move or hobby or new relationship." Those naysayers will become nothing more than noise; perhaps they'll even cease to play a role in your life. You have to have conviction in what you want to create for yourself, and it really doesn't matter what anyone else's opinion is, unless it directly hurts them.

> *"As long as a man stands in his own way,*
> *everything seems to be in his way."*
> — Ralph Waldo Emerson

Ever tried putting on a pair of rose-colored glasses and seeing the world through a different lens? Now's the time to do this.

Don't let your own past limitations, hurdles or failures limit what you are able to experience right here and now. Don't let those things impact your judgment or, more importantly, your expectations. Instead, think of how you want your life to be, and take the steps to put that life into place.

THE SKY'S THE LIMIT

Jenifer Kramer is an excellent example of someone who was able to do just that. With 100% intention, she decided, shortly after New

Year's Day, that the following year would be the best one of her life (so far). She was due for a great year. Her abusive father passed away on Jan. 1 the year before.

Six months later, at the age of 43, she learned he was not her biological father. A few weeks after that, she was diagnosed with Borderline Personality Disorder tendencies, and in December of that same year, she was hit by a car while standing on a sidewalk. Jenifer walked away from the accident without a single broken bone. She was struck by how precious life truly is.

Recovering from the accident and realizing how lucky she had been made her want never to take anything for granted again. To honor her profound experience, she started sharing gratitude posts on Facebook every day.

From that point forward, everything in her life changed. Her business thrived. She began to cut ties with people in her life who were not fulfilling her, and she started to take better care of herself.

> *"Never limit your view of life by any past experience."*
> — Ernest Holmes, *The Science of Mind*

Inspired by how just a few small changes could impact her entire outlook, Jenifer enrolled in a manifestation course. Things really took off from there. To kick-start her dreams for a new life, she decided to upgrade everything, starting with her living situation. After 14 years in the same apartment, she found a beautiful new home that was exactly within her budget and began to purge. She got rid of the things that no longer brought her joy and surrounded herself with things that brought her happiness.

Her manifestation group was a huge source of support as Jenifer went through the transition. She had a venue to share her successes and celebrate her wins. Jenifer says *the most surprising part of her Reinvention was how easy it was once she set the intention for a different kind of life.* She's thriving in her new home and her new skin, living in appreciation. The accident was the final straw in her old life, and she credits it with being her wake-up call to her life's potential.

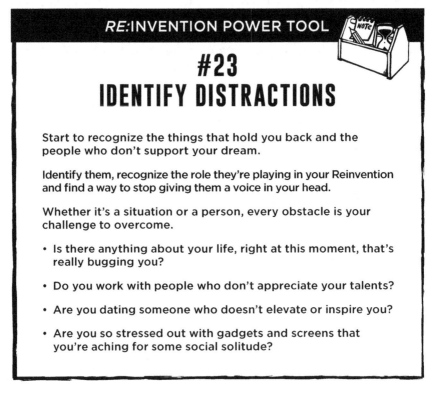

*RE:*INVENTION POWER TOOL

#23
IDENTIFY DISTRACTIONS

Start to recognize the things that hold you back and the people who don't support your dream.

Identify them, recognize the role they're playing in your Reinvention and find a way to stop giving them a voice in your head.

Whether it's a situation or a person, every obstacle is your challenge to overcome.

- Is there anything about your life, right at this moment, that's really bugging you?

- Do you work with people who don't appreciate your talents?

- Are you dating someone who doesn't elevate or inspire you?

- Are you so stressed out with gadgets and screens that you're aching for some social solitude?

DIG DEEPER:
ASSESS YOUR CHALLENGES

- Identify the challenges that are disabling the lifestyle you seek

- Isolate the challenges and learn to address them head on

- Analyze why and how they're impacting you

- Explore scenarios for minimizing and reducing these challenges

- Consider how you deal with the challenges when they come up and how you feel

- Use the "breaking habits" exercises presented in Chapter 8

- Come up with a list of options and solutions for changing the course

- Develop a list of ways to buffer and/or soften the feelings (take a walk, whistle, take a hot bath, call a friend, quit, break up, speak your mind, be honest with yourself)

- Know your worth and your capability as a human being (find someone to remind you if you've lost sight of it)

Whatever you're facing — whether you're too busy, too stressed, too bored, too uninspired — now is the time to reach for the "more." Do it! Pull out that notebook!

> *"One day you will wake up and there won't be any more time to do the things you've always wanted. Do it now."*
> — Paulo Coelho

THE TECHNOLOGY PARADOX

I often wonder how we functioned in the world without all the technology and interconnectivity we have today. The irony, of course, is the lack of connectivity we have to one another as human beings.

I grew up in the era of speaking to each other over meals, writing letters to friends across the world and waiting a painstaking two weeks to get one back. I recall running to the mailbox in anticipation of those letters that had the AIR MAIL stamp on blue paper-thin stationery within a self-folding envelope. (It was the dinosaur age, as my kids would say, back when we used typewriters!)

Our kids have different social norms, and their friendships live and die over social media. Meanwhile, the adults scramble to "keep up with the Joneses" on technology platforms. We can barely have a conversation without being pinged, happed or buzzed from some type of gadget that keeps our heads buried in our phones. Yet this digital world is supposed to make us more "connected"? Connected to what?

Technology's impact on the next generation (and even our own) is curious. It reminds me of the great debate around television, handheld game devices, walkmans, video games and even junk food. The solution was to teach our kids/selves to watch, listen, play or eat in moderation. Admittedly, social media and 24/7 smartphones make "modern moderation" very difficult.

We don't exercise our brains the way we used to, and, thus, there is a diminishing capacity to do as much as we are capable of doing. Our phones tell us when to go to sleep and when to wake up. They're with us when we brush our teeth and have our first morning coffee. We rely on them to get us from point A to point B. They monitor our heart rates, searching patterns, shopping habits and everything else we do throughout the day. Personally, I'd rather snuggle up to a warm body than a computer at night.

We don't rely on our minds as much, and we don't trust ourselves to remember the little things. Think about it. If you lost your phone, would you be able to get in touch with anyone you speak to on a regular basis? We used to memorize everyone's phone numbers and remembered them for years and years because they were ingrained in our memories.

The paradox is we're overusing our brains in one way as we multi-task, search, communicate and document everything we think, see and experience. Yet, we're not able to remember some of the simplest things, like what we need at the grocery store or what books are on our reading lists or when to make a vet appointment.

Our phones also help us to avoid reality. We escape the day-to-day by surfing other people's social media feeds. We're consumed all day and night by devices that don't make it any easier to slow down and rejuvenate. Our gadgets run out of juice, and so do we. We frantically search for places to plug in and charge our smartphones — if we don't, they won't serve us. *Ironic. We spend more time charging our gadgets than we do ourselves!*

Resist the urge to engage with the gadgets, and take the time to recharge your own battery. Know what makes you feel good, warm and fuzzy. Teach your children to cherish opportunities to let their imaginations run free. Walk down a street or around a school campus, and look at your fellow humans, make eye contact, smile, be engaged, be present. Just be.

Dare to unplug and explore your world — the one world you're living in, not the lives of people you used to know from high school when you scroll through their seemingly perfect vacations, concerts, meals and family time. Be open to hearing yourself, not everyone else. Sometimes the grass *really is greener.* And you'll find it only when you open the door and step outside.

Before you say you don't have time, think about the amount of time you'd have if you pushed the phone and computer away just a little more — reprioritize. Don't believe me? Log your hours for two weeks and see.

Give it a try. What are you waiting for?

CHAPTER 14

IT'S NOT A MIDLIFE CRISIS.
IT'S A CRY FOR *RE:*INVENTION.

"The good life is a process,
not a state of being.
It is a direction,
not a destination."

— Carl Rogers

That itchy restlessness, boredom and frustration that kicks in sometime in our mid-30s through late 50s is often referred to as a midlife crisis. I'll go so far as to argue that, whatever is going on with you, *it's not a midlife crisis; it's a cry for Reinvention. This chapter is dedicated to all the people who feel like the only way out of this headspace is to go off the deep end.*

Listen! You don't need to blow up your life, trade in the station wagon for a red convertible Porsche or dive into a damaging extramarital affair to overcome the feelings and frustrations associated with midlife. All you need to do is make a few small changes.

MEN DON'T ASK FOR DIRECTIONS

Both men and women are guilty of dramatic and often destructive coping mechanisms. But at least women talk to each other in greater depth about what is going on in their lives and with their feelings.

When men go through the rough spots, they tend to retreat into their caves or into silence. They don't reach out, they don't communicate, they convert that energy into anger and restlessness and their testosterone multiplies. A midlife crisis only perpetuates the problem.

Women, on the other hand, have a community. They lift one another up and provide a powerful resource for each other to explore, problem-solve, share, excite, encourage and engage.

We need to teach our men (friends, husbands, siblings) how to leverage this special gift — whether we give them more of it or invite them into our world a little more.

The old adage "Men don't ask for directions" is such a great metaphor for why *I decided to write this book for men as well as women. I was repeatedly asked/told to make it a women's book. In my usual style, I've held my ground and zagged when others are zigging in the women's support movement.* Men just won't reach out when they need to. They don't work out the process and solutions the way that women do. *Men need inspiration and permission to Reinvent almost more than women.* The pressure and expectations over the generations make it hard for them to shed their traditional roles of shouldering the family and financial responsibilities. Thus, the "go to work"/"be accountable"/"do your job"/"protect and serve the family" roles need to be tweaked.

Not only are men wired differently, but between the silenced emotions and the lack of communication, they're not going to get where they need to go to get unstuck, which is not fair! Women need to step up and offer access to the community.

"

THIS BOOK IS FOR ALL THE MEN OUT
THERE WHO ARE SEEKING A ROAD MAP,
EVEN THOUGH THEY
DIDN'T ASK FOR ONE!

The midlife blues do not have to become a full-blown crisis unless you let them. Likely, your soul is crying out for a Reinvention, but it doesn't have to be epic to have an impact. There are effective ways to add a layer of joy to your life that will make whatever you're facing easier to overcome. Scott and his violin playing, which we discussed in an earlier chapter, is a great example of this.

A STUDENT OF LIFE

Can a 50-plus-year-old man find a home among 800+ millennials? James Orsini brought years of experience and wisdom to a conversation we shared recently about when he met Gary Vaynerchuk, CEO of Vayner Media. It was four years ago. James was 51 years old.

The question James asked himself before they met, in this day of overly confident and cutting-edge, bright millennials, was "Would there be a place for him at Vayner Media, one of the hottest new digital marketing agencies on Madison Ave." He didn't have the tech and digital experience the young whippersnappers had, and he would need a crash course in digital marketing.

Apparently, the answer was "Yes." There *was* a place for him. Gary had the wisdom to recognize the fortitude, gravitas and skills James brought to his own dreams and vision and wanted a man who could be his #2, which in James's book, was the #1 position he wanted.

With a humble but precocious nature, a background as a CEO, CFO and corporate entrepreneur who had witnessed the evolution of the media, brand, promotion, PR and technology landscape over the last three decades, there was no question that James was the man for this job.

He had just finished a three-year employment contract as CEO of a small, publicly traded mobile media company when James heard about

Gary V. A colleague told him if he ever found an opportunity to work for a man like Gary — a visionary — to jump on it. James did.

He says the Ah-Ha Moment came during their first dinner together. Gary asked him to describe what he does in one sentence. James answered, "I take dreams and visions and turn them into action plans." Gary said, "Well, I have a lot of dreams and visions. You're hired!"

A book called *Consigliere: Leading From the Shadows* by Richard Hytner — about being a great #2 — confirmed that James' decision spoke to his sweet spot! Validation that you're on the right path is a great thing to discover.

For his Reinvention, James embarked on one of the wildest rides of his life. He had to be relevant to the young people at the company as well as relatable and approachable. He also realized he had to be more open minded than ever. Of his new role, he says, "I do a lot more listening now. I filter more, digest more and then formulate opinions applying modern thought processes and technology to 30 years of financial and operational business acumen."

Training on the job was critical. As an evolving student of life and business, James learned that "Content and Attention Are King" in his business. He learned to blog on Medium and has been doing podcast interviews, speaking engagements and utilizing social media to the point he impresses his own kids!

Mentoring the younger generation of emerging business leaders is another valuable part of James's world. Always thinking, always evaluating options for growth and evolution is imperative to keeping him invigorated and feeling alive in what he does.

James has embraced the millennial generation he works with and recognizes he's gotten a better understanding of them. He says: "They are much more than most people of my generation give them credit for.

They are collaborative, engaged, fearless and eager to learn." Apparently, the same can be said for James — the 55-year-old Reinventor who is now the President of the newly formed Sasha Group for Vayner Media.

EMPTY NESTERS

One of the most common midlife events that tend to trigger a strong "OMG. What am I doing with my life?" moment is when the kids fly the coop. Whether they head off to college or to a job, being without your children can lead to anxiety for a lot of different reasons, not to mention trigger a midlife crisis.

I love being a mom: feeling needed and wanted, nurturing and care-taking while constantly in awe of the amazing little people that turn into grown-up human beings — whom *we* created! It never ceases to amaze me and give me such incredible joy.

I was an empty nester for about four months — much shorter than I expected. My oldest son went away to school, and we saw him several times a year. But when it was time for my younger son to head off on his college journey, the thought of the house being empty made me sad. Raising my sons had been the greatest years of my life, and I wasn't ready for the new life ahead of me, even though we all see it coming. I wasn't 100% sure what it would be like when my husband and I had the house to ourselves again. It hadn't been "just us" for 21 years!

Alas, my younger son didn't love his Midwest college experience and after much deliberation (there's a whole other book on that one) came home after the first semester to go to college locally until he figured out his next move. Just as we were getting used to the notion of having our lives back and feeling like we were 24 and playing house again . . . the kid came back! Thank goodness we love him so much and love having him around.

Nevertheless, many of the connotations of an empty nest are negative and come with a huge dose of sadness. Our babies have moved on, and they leave us holding . . . memories. Memories of the most beautiful, challenging, emotional, happy, special and life-changing moments ever.

For some, the empty nest is a time of celebration — to have the house back to yourself, to do what you want when you want, to be free from day-to-day care-taking responsibilities. No more late-night trips to the market to make sure the basic necessities are in the fridge to feed your kids, and, God forbid, you have to make cookies for that bake-sale fundraiser at midnight while you're on a business deadline! No more yelling at them to clean up their rooms or waiting up until 1 a.m. to hear the front door close quietly behind them, or dragging them out of bed to make the bus or making their friends get their feet off the coffee table.

Now those daily hugs and face-to-face conversations have transformed into texts, FaceTime calls and expensive plane tickets. So many of my friends are going through this horrible/terrific transition/Reinvention as their kids leave/give them space to go off to school/parents' timeout.

So, yes, we'll miss those kids when they leave, and we wonder how to get by without them.

So just consider this for a moment . . .

What are you going to do with all those extra hours? And your newfound lack of responsibilities?

This is your opportunity to take back some of your old life and return to the time when you wondered what you could do to make your life more full and complete — the time when you reveled in thoughts of your own personal indulgences, hobbies and creative passions. One way or another, we've all wondered what we would do with a little more time if we weren't so busy raising our kids. Would we expand our careers, find a passion we could turn into a job or find a hobby that nurtured our souls?

> *"I'd rather regret the things I've done*
> *than regret the things I haven't . . ."*
> — Lucille Ball

What would you do if you had a little extra time on your hands or needed to find something to fill that now-missing piece of time in your life?

---

*RE:*INVENTION POWER TOOL

#24
NOW WHAT? RECLAIM YOUR LIFE!

Guess what? With the kids out of the house, there are no more excuses! So:

- Reconnect with your spouse

- Put on those running shoes

- Go buy that garden shovel

- Tell your boss how you feel about your job so you can get that promotion

- Clean out and redo one of the kids' rooms

- Do that volunteer work

- Call up those friends you've been pushing aside for years

- Take back your weekends, and do something fun

- Make those travel plans with your friends and loved ones

- Visit some remote part of the city

- Be a tourist in your own hometown . . .

Are you getting the picture?

"

THE RALLYING CRY OF EMPTY
NESTERS IS THE MATING CALL FOR
REINVENTION.

This is *your* time, again. Use it wisely. Love your children, make sure they're doing well, and support them growing into great people, but, also, show them how it's done and what's possible in life!

Modeling a Reinvention is an amazing way for your kids to see that we should *never* stop exploring the world, our interests, our passions. Their years in college are just the beginning of testing out life as adults and learning about things they never even knew existed. Be an example to them from afar.

I remember taking courses in college such as Astronomy, Archaeology, Sociology of Deviant Behavior, Middle Eastern Studies, Public Speaking, Film Studies and Philosophy. These are the courses that I constantly recall, even though I was a Communications major, because I gained exposure to things I might not ever experience or learn again. Those classes made an impression on me. It was my time to explore — and guess what? It's that time again . . . right now! I may not be in college, but there's an entire world to discover.

Our journey is just beginning again, so rethink those tough moments. Don't be sad or anxious that your kids aren't around: seize the moment, and dig deep. What are your passions, and how are you going to live this one incredible life?

DON'T GET DIVORCED — GET BUSY

Some people want to blame their unhappiness in a relationship on their spouse. They find ways to pick on them, or they look at the glass half-empty rather than half-full in their relationship. They find all the reasons they can to blame their partner for everything they didn't accomplish on their own "dream" list. But, take a closer look. Is it really true? *Who do you hold accountable for your choices?*

I know in my relationship there's a healthy amount of love, trust and respect mixed in with the occasional fight or disagreement. One thing I'm certain of is that we've given each other the space to pursue the things we love to do. I might blame him that I can't get to the gym because I have to make dinner, run errands with him on a Saturday or something else that "got in the way." But if I'm truly honest, I know how quickly those excuses take over. *It's a lot easier to play the blame game than accept responsibility. When I really want to go to Yoga or Zumba, I do, and dinner can wait, or the errands can get done without me. That's the truth.*

So, who's really to blame when you aren't fulfilling your dreams or making time for the activities you care about? *You* have to hold *yourself* accountable for *your own happiness.*

It might be time to revisit the notion that your partner is holding you back. Pursue all that makes *you happy* on your Reinvention, and stop being angry with someone else. Once you're engaged with your newfound dream or pursuit, you may find your spouse is there to support you in ways you never thought possible, because you never gave them the chance to.

Perhaps your relationship will thrive due to a new level of respect, admiration and love. Perhaps setting the intention to "get busy" and follow your own heart might just be the thing that saves your marriage. Seems worth the effort to me.

EVERY DAY IS THE FIRST DAY OF THE REST OF YOUR LIFE

So you've been thinking, contemplating, ideating, saying you're going to make that one little change or that huge leap, but, so far, it's just noise in your head.

What's stopping you? Are you going to have to give up something that you're not prepared to do without, or are you simply content within your comfort zone? These are legitimate reasons for not moving forward.

However, it's worthwhile to consider the rewards of the idea you've been considering. What's the upside?

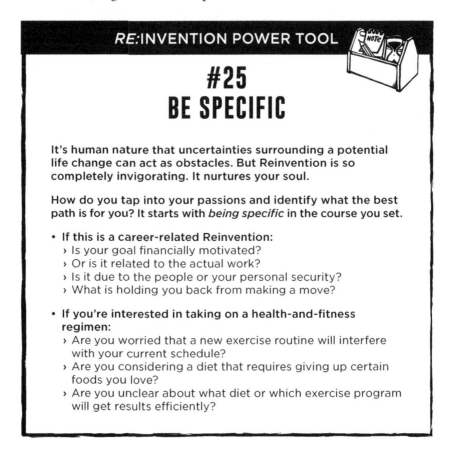

*RE:*INVENTION POWER TOOL

#25
BE SPECIFIC

It's human nature that uncertainties surrounding a potential life change can act as obstacles. But Reinvention is so completely invigorating. It nurtures your soul.

How do you tap into your passions and identify what the best path is for you? It starts with *being specific* in the course you set.

- **If this is a career-related Reinvention:**
  › Is your goal financially motivated?
  › Or is it related to the actual work?
  › Is it due to the people or your personal security?
  › What is holding you back from making a move?

- **If you're interested in taking on a health-and-fitness regimen:**
  › Are you worried that a new exercise routine will interfere with your current schedule?
  › Are you considering a diet that requires giving up certain foods you love?
  › Are you unclear about what diet or which exercise program will get results efficiently?

If you're to have any hope of accomplishing your goals, you have to detail what you're setting out to do and what steps you need to take to get there. You need to understand the why's/why not's, which are the great motivators to accomplishing anything.

For example: you want to Reinvent a piece of your life that will make you feel healthier and more in control of how you feel every day. You know you're not getting any younger, so anything you do to improve your health is a win-win. So "improved health" is your goal.

Now, write down the things that you can do *every day* to improve your health — starting with the easy things.

Be specific. Your list may look something like this:

1. Vitamins. Introduce them into your daily routine.

   • Go to the health-food store, talk to the salesperson, and ask what's best for you, your age and your specific health conditions. Share what other medications you're taking. Check with your doctor if necessary.

   • Put your new vitamins in your bathroom or on your desk — somewhere you won't forget to take them every day.

   • Put a daily reminder on your calendar until it becomes habit.

2. Exercise regimen. Start one, or add something new. If you've been inactive, start with something attainable that doesn't cost a lot. *Be specific* about your fitness goals.

   • Load up your iPod with podcasts or music you love that gets you moving.

   • Commit to taking a walk three times a week (at minimum), or establish a new power workout that is a step up from what you've been doing. Perhaps look into a dance class. Zumba is all the rage. Give it a shot — it's a blast!

- Put your walking or workout dates and times on your calendar — make an appointment with yourself, and don't cancel!

- Every few weeks, add another level of activity — e.g., 50–100 sit-ups 4 times a week.

3. Food. Stop eating "something" today.

- Right now, pick one item you'll eliminate for the next three days: bread, pasta, sugar, salt — you pick. *Be specific,* and stick to it. It's not forever, just a few days. When the mental and physical rewards kick in, you'll be more motivated to do it longer.

4. Water. Commit to drinking at least eight tall glasses a day.

- Set the times you will drink your water. Don't just leave it to a general commitment, or you'll get to the end of a day and suddenly realize you have to drink five glasses before bed!

- Carry a bottle of water around with you like it's your new best friend.

Now you can take this level of specificity and apply it to anything — picking up a new hobby, switching careers, redecorating your home, rejoining the workforce, a spiritual Reinvention.

Be realistic, so that you can achieve success and reward the baby steps. The more you do this, the more motivated you will be to do more.

"Happiness is a habit. Cultivate it."
— Elbert Hubbard

"

IF YOU FEEL GOOD ABOUT
YOURSELF AND WHAT YOU CAN DO
FOR YOURSELF, EVERYTHING ELSE
YOU WANT TO TACKLE
WILL FEEL SURMOUNTABLE.

There's always a way through the crisis. As they say, "It's always darkest before the dawn" — *and this is your dawn* — *your moment of discovery when you realize that what you thought was a bad time in your life is really a moment to reflect, re-center and reset your course of Reinvention.* Midlife is a time that puts *you* at the center of your own life.

Aren't you worth the effort?

PART 5:
INSPIRATION

CHAPTER 15:

THE TIPPING POINT

"Let life happen to you. Believe me: life is in the right, always."
— Rainer Maria Rilke

While this book is about making our Reinvention "happen," there are countless situations when Reinvention "happens to us." This occurs in the form of losing a job, a loved one, your savings or maybe even losing your mind. I've already shared several stories of people who were faced with an unexpected loss or surprise that prompted a Reinvention.

It could happen in the form of questioning our sexuality, facing a health crisis or discovering a hard truth about an important relationship. Indeed, none of us are immune to tragedy. It's not something you can hide from or hide behind. Instead, you need to process it, feel it, and move through it to emerge on the other side an even stronger, smarter, wiser person even more committed to your own life.

Nothing fuels a Reinvention like defeat. Indeed, *in times of tragedy, it is important to remain open.*

Some of my favorite Reinvention stories are from folks who landed firmly on their butts in their careers, in their love lives or in the public eye — and who stood up, dusted themselves off and emerged with a new sense of self-worth and identity that they never imagined possible. We must realize that, every day, each and every one of us is at our own personal crossroads, and it's up to us whether we leverage the moment or settle for the path of least resistance.

Tragedy forces us to find the courage to push through. And while it would be challenging to offer "tools" to help you with unplanned-for challenges, I can absolutely offer some inspirational stories of Reinventions that occurred because of them.

The stories in this chapter are proof that the light really is stronger than the darkness and that no tragedy should ever have the power to define who or what we become. I hope they inspire you the same way they inspired me.

> *"Life is either daring adventure or nothing."*
> — Helen Keller

LEAP. LIVE.

I have a friend who used a tragedy as a catalyst to go all in on the experience of living. Amy Lorbati's loss was overwhelming, but it was also a gift. Her brother's sudden death triggered her to get to work on her own life Reinvention. Confronted with the reality that life can be taken at any moment, she realized she didn't want to be one of those people who sits around saying, "I wish I would have done XYZ." She saw her life ahead and wanted to make it the best possible one she could.

Shortly after her brother died, Amy started to show up on Facebook in weird and interesting places, doing daring and adventurous things. I was blown away and wondered how she had the time (she was working full-time). Let alone the courage (solo traveling to foreign countries) and the passion (exploring Europe on the back of a motorcycle). Amy wasn't messing around. No grass was going to grow under her feet. Her brother would have been proud!

"Leap, and the net will appear."

— John Burroughs

But Amy didn't restrict her newfound sense of adventure to travel. Her "I dare me" attitude trickled into her home life as well. She overhauled her duplex from an older, darker, average space into a new, white, open and light area. She called in her cavalry of friends and designers, who gave her apartment an entire reboot with just a little paint and some new furniture.

She went for it in all directions, and her life blossomed into an extraordinary bright, beautiful canvas. She started exploring the world, including a lengthy stay in the beauty of Thailand, all while studying to become a transformational life coach. She left the entertainment industry, sold her house in Hollywood and moved to a mountain community outside of Los Angeles. She is launching her dream business and reprioritizing the way she's living her life, surrounded by love, spirituality and a healthy dose of zen!

But you don't have to overhaul your life and tick off your entire Bucket List to start a Reinvention. *One small change can create such a huge shift in your energy, your surroundings, the way you connect with other people, your moods. You're sending a signal to those around you and to the universe that you are open and interested in creating the best possible life.*

The truth is, there are numerous opportunities for a better, more fulfilling life staring all of us in the face right at this very moment, yet most of us won't take the risk of harnessing those opportunities. Why? We're complacent. We're comfortable.

"

IT ISN'T UNTIL SOMETHING
CHANGES — WE GET LAID OFF,
WE GET OLDER, WE LOSE SOMEONE
WE RELIED UPON — THAT WE REALIZE
HOW STRONG AND AMAZING
WE TRULY ARE.

Reinvention is about recognizing those blessings in disguise that force us to stand taller than we ever thought possible and, in turn, push our lives to new and greater heights. It's about embracing rejection, loss, failure and all of the ugly things we try to outrun on a daily basis and realizing that sometimes they are the foundation for a new and better life.

It's not always easy to embrace adversity in this way. Our initial reaction might be to curl up in the fetal position in our closet or keep the blinds drawn for a few days (weeks, months) before we're ready to face the change that lies before us. But for those who do it, who muster the strength to Reinvent and redefine their concept of success, the results are big time.

We will all experience defeat. In the end, as with most things, it is about choice. It's about the way we choose to face our challenges and how we choose to define ourselves, and what lessons we take from our failures. *No matter what happens in life, we are always at choice.*

I DIDN'T MEAN TO *RE:*INVENT

Death of a loved one is often a catalyst for change. Many have shared stories with me on this topic. It's a recurring theme.

It was on the day her father died when Lori Geller — she was 33 years old at the time — discovered she was an artist. In a fit of grief, she hid in the bathroom while her family soundly slept. In need of an outlet for her pain and without thinking, she pulled a crumpled deli napkin from the trash, grabbed a pencil, and drew what would be her first piece of art: nothing more than a perfect square, immaculate in its shape and as perfect as her father.

With purpose, she says, she drew a single triangle in the lower right quadrant of the square, grabbed a cuticle scissor from the drawer and proceeded to cut the simple triangle out of it — a space that, to her, represented the empty place in her heart once filled by her father.

That simple sketch led her to reproduce a three-dimensional structure of the sketch out of solid wood to symbolize her father's strength. She then hung the square in her living room and the small, seemingly lost, triangle on a beam of the living-room ceiling. This first piece was painted in Ferrari red paint to show the love in her heart for her dad.

It wasn't until 2003, when a friend saw the work and requested a reproduction for her Palm Springs home, that Lori realized she might be onto something special. Soon after, an art gallery in Palm Desert displayed her collection, and her life as an artist truly started.

Lori's work is now featured internationally. Her success is based solely on word of mouth. Her works have been displayed in New York at the Time Warner Center, at the Museum of Contemporary Art in Los Angeles and in other museum collections around the world. None of it would have happened if it hadn't been for the loss of her father.

In Lori's case, her tragedy exposed a new and wonderful talent. But tragedy can also empower us to redefine what is most important in our lives.

Beauty is born of destruction. History has proven it time and time again. Nations unite in times of national tragedy. Families find one another following the loss of a loved one or friend. Often it takes pain to put things into a greater perspective.

Don't let your own past limitations, hurdles or failures limit your expectations of what you are able to experience right here and now. As they say, *what you expect, you experience. Sometimes when life breaks things apart, it allows us to rebuild ourselves — and our lives — even stronger.* Try to see the opportunity in every life change, and you will undoubtedly find yourself on the most amazing — and amazingly unexpected — adventure.

"

FLOWERS REALLY DO RISE AFTER
THE RAIN, AND MOST OF THE TIME,
THEY ARE EVEN MORE BEAUTIFUL
AND RESILIENT THAN BEFORE
THE STORM BEGAN.

"I am bigger than anything that can happen to me. All these things, sorrow, misfortune and suffering, are outside my door. I am in the house, and I have the key."

— Charles Fletcher Lummis

YOUR FAILURE CAN BE YOUR *BIGGEST* SUCCESS

Marci Freedman didn't need to tell me her Reinvention story. I knew it intimately, because I was right there in her life when it happened. In fact, it's still happening, and it's been a joyous celebration to watch her make lemonade out of the lemons she was handed.

Marci's marketing career has been populated by some huge industry names — Mattel, Reebok, vitaminwater and Coca Cola among them. Of her unexpected Reinvention, Marci says:

"My world completely shifted when I was recruited (after eight years) to leave one of the best jobs in America, Director of Lifestyle Marketing at vitaminwater, to oversee marketing as SVP of a small investment group in NYC. I was having a hard time making a smart decision, so I consulted a career coach, who said, 'Your new boss is handing you a gift, and you need to take it.' So, after eight incredible years of building that brand, I gave my notice, packed up my convertible and never looked back!

After two great years, the investment group went into Chapter 7, taking 80 people down with it, and my world imploded. All the fear, failure and frustration came rushing in, and I spiraled. I couldn't understand how all this had happened or where I was going to go next.

I had always worn my jobs as 'badges,' which wasn't hard to do because, in my mind, I had the greatest jobs. I was 'The

Reebok Girl' or 'The vitaminwater Girl.' I was scared that, without a corporate name or a hot job to identify with, people would forget about me. I had to stay in the game! But what would that look like?

With a little clarity and distance, I realized I didn't want to go back to being a corporate robot. *I was going to bet on myself and become my own boss.* I wouldn't take on any new clients or business if it didn't fit into my 6 Ps:

- Product (I have to believe in it and be a consumer)

- People (The founder must be a rock star with a strong vision)

- Passion (Do I care deeply about what the company is doing?)

- Packaging (Is it creative/disruptive?)

- Personality (Is the brand distinctive, or have some sizzle?)

- Purpose (What does the company stand for?)

I would wear my 'Marci Freedman' badge and come back better, stronger, more mature and more grounded than I had ever been before. I am the brand and will work with companies and in industries that I am super passionate about. It became less about the title and money and more about my happiness and work/life balance. I created this beautiful imaginary toolkit and haven't stopped putting things into it professionally and personally. And there began my spiritual journey, which led me onto my happiness path.

What I thought was the biggest failure of my life led to my biggest success. The most surprising aspect of being independent has been all of the things I've said *Yes* to that in the past would have been *No* or *Never*. My Reinvention has taught me to live differently, more minimally. There is much less noise in my life now, and I love it."

Marci is living her "True North." She's confident owning her space and choosing to live life on her terms, not those of others. She is a light and a force in the lives of all those around her and is a lesson in how to transition gracefully.

"I didn't see it then, but it turned out that getting fired from Apple was the best thing that could have ever happened to me. The heaviness of being successful was replaced by the lightness of being a beginner again . . . It freed me to enter one of the most creative periods of my life."

— Steve Jobs

When one door closes, another opens. Sometimes when we're in the thick of it, it's hard to see that with optimism and enthusiasm. If you start to understand the opportunity, embrace the time for change and use some of the Power Tools we've been discussing, you might move through this stage of your life with focus, clarity and determination — armed with a plan.

CHAPTER 16:
SERIAL *RE:*INVENTIONS

"The straight line,
a respectable optical illusion which ruins many a man."
— Victor Hugo, *Les Misérables*

Sometimes, one Reinvention just isn't enough to fulfill us. We realize we aren't meant for living life in a straight line. Like rolling stones, our hearts are alight with the thought of constant movement and change. For these souls, I have coined the phrase, "Serial Reinventors."

Some of my favorite friends and well-known celebrities are just these types of Renaissance men and women. They're people who didn't settle for being just one thing: a singer, an Olympian, an actor, a model, a director, a lawyer, an agent, a mom. They didn't settle for just one style or image. They have too much life and inspiration within them to limit it to one single direction. They experienced success in one arena and felt the need to move on.

*"We are going to relentlessly chase perfection, knowing full well
we will not catch it, because nothing is perfect. But we are
going to relentlessly chase it, because, in the process,
we will catch excellence. I am not remotely
interested in just being good."*
— Vince Lombardi

For me, the most inspiring thing about serial Reinventing is that it provides hope to all of us that *change, in and of itself, is OK. It's OK to change our minds and reverse our outlooks. It's OK to make the "wrong" decision (meaning, a decision that is no longer "right" in this moment).* We will survive. And we can even be happy and successful while we're changing course.

Of course, there are also valuable lessons to be learned from our Serial Reinventors. It probably goes without saying that life changes don't always go as planned. *This chapter is dedicated to all of those fluttering hearts . . . those rolling stones whose feet dare not stop moving.* Their lessons in faith and love are treasure maps for all of us. They inspire me daily with their willingness to leap into the great unknown.

*"I've experienced great things; I've experienced great
tragedies. I've done almost everything I could possibly ever
imagine doing, but I just know that there's more."*
— Dave Grohl

DREAMS CHANGE AS YOU CHANGE

Due to the economic climate in 2008, Lori Sale opted for an early retirement. After years in a high-paying job in the entertainment industry, she felt ground down and disillusioned, and it was time to move

"

AFTER ALL, THE ONLY CERTAINTY
IN LIFE IS CHANGE. OUR INTERESTS
CHANGE. OUR FRIENDS CHANGE. WE
MEET NEW PEOPLE WHO INSPIRE
US WITH WHAT THEY HAVE
EXPERIENCED AND SEEN IN THE
WORLD. WE WANT NEW THINGS
OUT OF LIFE. WE GROW OUT OF ONE
SELF AND REINVENT ANOTHER.

on. She made sure her team were well taken care of when she left, so she could sleep at night.

As soon as her retirement began, Lori felt like a fish out of water. Her working friends were preoccupied and stressed, and she struggled to connect with her non-working friends. Her kids were old enough that they didn't need her as much as they once had, and as she told me, "You can go to the gym for only so long every day."

Lori tried a slew of new activities to occupy her time: golf, tennis and cooking lessons. Nothing stuck, and she was going nuts. She was driving her husband crazy, too. One day, he finally said, "What are you going to do? You're not wired to sit around idle. You have so many great ideas; pick one, and go do it."

After three weeks of "retirement," she decided to open a studio/dry bar based on a back-pocket Reinvention fantasy she'd had for a while. She dug into the Internet and taught herself what she needed to know to open a retail space. She also lost a lot of sleep in the process, worrying that she would drive her family into financial ruin, that no one would come into her store, that her idea was a bad one.

Although she was already an entrepreneur, a major power broker and a serious dealmaker, the dry bar was a new field with a lot of unknowns. She gave herself a crash course in how to raise money, negotiate a lease, become a retail buyer and run a successful solo business. But the most important thing she learned throughout the experience of planning, opening and operating her new business: she didn't really love owning and operating a beauty bar.

Soon after starting her venture, she realized she missed the adrenaline rush of being an entertainment agent. She was driven by the hundreds of daily emails and calls she used to receive and the feeling of being needed and brokering power deals. The retail experience didn't give her the same sense of satisfaction at the end of the day, and it was time to move on and contemplate the next step.

Lori has an adventurous personality, and she was happy to try something new. For some, accepting that their dream didn't "work out" might be more difficult. In her case, after some thoughtful contemplation and a little time off, she wound up returning to the entertainment space, where she felt right at home. With all her years of experience, maturity and new focus, she returned to her earlier roots of running her own agency. She created a new company that enabled her to utilize her inherent skills, and the business was fueled by her intense drive to succeed. The thriving business and her balanced life are exactly where she belongs.

Lori allowed herself to explore these Reinventions with the intention of always moving forward, which is precisely what's possible when you put your mind to it. Her experience with Reinvention was a success in so many ways. She learned a lot about business and herself, and she was able to work her way through several business ideas when she made the decision to leave her job in the first place.

> *"I've just entered my second — no, actually third — wait,*
> *probably fourth — act. I'm not a hobby person. My*
> *interest is and always has been working."*
> — Lori Sale

WHAT'S NEXT?

Another one of my favorite serial Reinvention inspirations is Robin Cousins, the 1980 Olympic Gold Medal Figure Skater for Great Britain. He knew before he got there that he was going to use whatever the Olympic experience gave him and build/learn from it, successful or not.

After he won the Gold Medal at the age of 22, he built an extraordinary life beyond the victory. The Olympic experience was more than he had wished for. Not only was he able to do something he loved every day, he represented his country on an international stage (twice). Rather than resting on his laurels after the win, he challenged himself to Reinvent his life.

When I spoke to Robin about his journey, he said, *"Winning an Olympic Gold Medal turned out to be a phenomenal way to end one chapter of my life and launch the next 40!* We all have choices . . . and mine was not to be defined by what people thought I should be or do because of my achievement. After the Olympics, my thought was, 'What's next?'"

Robin's personal philosophy has always been to "Put yourself out there. All you can do is ask the questions. What's the worst thing that can happen?" He says, *"I would rather hear the word 'No' from someone else than to have to ask myself, 'What if?'"*

His spirit of continual Reinvention led Robin to a diverse and exciting, ever-shifting career. Instead of suppressing his childhood curiosities, he developed the passion he had as a boy for musical theatre and performed on stage in London's West End in shows like *Cats, Grease, The Rocky Horror Show* and *Chicago*. He has performed around the world for hundreds and thousands of people doing something he loves. He's taught and choreographed emerging Olympians whose ambitions were as simple as his own were as a young boy.

He has also created and co-produced television specials for major networks on both sides of the Atlantic. For more than 35 years, he's been commentating for figure-skating events for the BBC.

Despite these accomplishments, Robin's not done yet. A Serial Reinventor at heart, he says, "There are still things out there for me to have a go at." And he says that, although the Olympic medal certainly opened a lot of doors, he probably would have either found the keys or banged those doors down anyway.

A BODY IN MOTION STAYS IN MOTION

My friend's mom, Ilene Sykes, has a similar thirst for change and spirit for creative Reinvention. She began her professional career out of college as a trainee in corporate retailing for Macy's. She worked for the company for ten years, eight of which she was a buyer. Ilene had the distinction of being the youngest buyer for the corporation but also the less-glamorous reality of being the lowest paid.

When her husband was transferred to Boston, she transitioned into executive recruitment and placement for the department store. She balanced this career move with teaching college-level retailing. After several more moves, becoming a stay-at-home mom and volunteering at the local library, Ilene earned a Master of Library Science degree at the age of 40.

Soon after she landed a permanent position in her new field, she and her husband bought a small chain of party-goods stores. The couple needed her retail acumen to launch the venture, so she split her time between being a librarian and wearing the CFO cap for the retail chain. Eventually, she let the librarian position go when the demands of the chain stores became too great.

Ilene was happy to have a variety of interests and skill sets, always learning and exploring within her fields. Her ultimate challenge and call for Reinvention came again in 2012, when she and her husband closed their business. He was ready for retirement, but Ilene decidedly was not.

She explored her options and found an unappealing employment landscape for someone her age. After scratching the surface, her long-term New York Life insurance agent and close friend asked if she might be interested in becoming an agent. The idea clicked. Thankfully, the local office had a new manager who was able to think outside the box. He found a spot for her in the three-year training program, and Ilene threw herself into the insurance world with both feet.

Of her later-in-life career transition, Ilene says, "My Ah-Ha Moment was when I realized that I could do anything I wanted: use my skills, retrain my brain, use my life skills, compete with anyone and be successful!! Why not?"

In her first year, she was the most successful new agent in office history. She qualified for Executive Council recognition (a very big deal) and passed her Series 6 and 63 financial-service exams (also a very big deal). Her career is taking off, she's her own boss and she makes more money than she imagined she would.

Her favorite part of the job, though, is her clients. She loves taking care of them, and all her combined life skills have led her to where she is today, working harder than ever before, and loving every minute of it.

Ilene's story inspires me beyond words. I smile whenever I think about her incredible perseverance and passion for Serial Reinvention.

"It's never too late — never too late to start
over, never too late to be happy."
— Jane Fonda

CHAPTER 17

THE *RE:*INVENTION ROAD MAP

"If not now, then when? If not you, then who?"
— Robin Sharma

This book is filled with tips and exercises to get you started on your Reinvention, but some of you may still wonder how on earth to move off square one.

This is one of the biggest dilemmas I often hear. "I am ready to Reinvent, but I don't know what to do!" Lack of clarity can be paralyzing.

My big goal for this book is to encourage everyone who reads it to take one step forward. Dip a toe in the water, imagine what's on the other side and dive in. Your life is waiting.

"If we continue to do what we've always done, we'll continue to get what we've always gotten."
— Anonymous

THE REINVENTION ROAD MAP IN 10 STEPS

Reinventions are incredible journeys, and they need mapping out, just as if you were going on a vacation or travelling somewhere new and interesting. They will be as successful and fulfilling as you allow yourself to make them.

Throughout the book, I've touched on a few of these topics briefly through stories and exercises. Now, for the purpose of presenting you with a simple, 10-Step Reinvention Road Map, the core concepts are laid out here.

You'll want to grab your notebook again. Look back on the ideas you've already jotted down and *dig deep*.

Step 1: Find your passion — the things that make your heart sing.

Step 2: Decide if you want to monetize it or simply engage in it and enjoy your new journey.

Step 3: Make a plan in stages that work for you: 1 week, 1 month, 6 months, 1 year. Maybe it's a 5-minute plan; maybe it's a 5-year plan. It can happen every single day if you let it. Whatever works and whatever gets you started. Baby steps! Break it down into manageable pieces.

Whether it's days or even years, a gradual transition is required. For example: Tuesday night — research subject xyz; Saturday afternoon — meet with an expert; Wednesday morning — attend networking breakfast.

Step 4: Set your goals — financial, emotional, physical, spiritual. Journal and make lists to hold yourself accountable. Review your goals regularly to make sure you are on track!

Step 5: Do the research — ask questions, talk to people, read blog posts, watch YouTube videos and explore the subject before digging in.

Step 6: Identify mentors — no one said you had to change your life on your own. One of the best ways to ensure a successful Reinvention is to find a mentor or support group to guide you through it. These are real people, with real experience and knowledge. Learn as much as you can from them, and hold them close as you work toward your goals.

Step 7: Assess the skills required — locate the resources to further your education, and seek out conferences, events, lectures and newsletters, and surround yourself with like-minded people.

Step 8: Immerse yourself in the subject matter — via interning or volunteering. "Try it on" to see if it really resonates with you and is worth the deeper dive and the effort you'll be putting into it.

Step 9: Get to it! Take small steps if you need to, and most definitely *reward yourself* for each accomplishment in your journey. Remember, Rome wasn't built in a day, and neither does your Reinvention need to be! (More on this in the next Power Tool.)

Step 10: Be prepared to modify your plan when needed. Change can be flexible, so don't quit if you hit a roadblock or if it's sitting there for too long; reassess the journey, the plan and the dream, and make your plan fit so you can achieve your goals.

Be flexible, and allow the evolution to occur. Most importantly, don't allow yourself to be overwhelmed by challenges. View them as learning experiences, and take them for what they're worth!

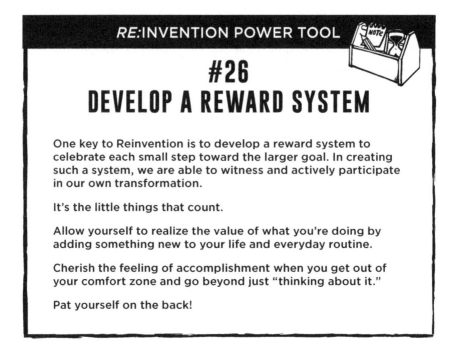

*RE:*INVENTION POWER TOOL

#26
DEVELOP A REWARD SYSTEM

One key to Reinvention is to develop a reward system to celebrate each small step toward the larger goal. In creating such a system, we are able to witness and actively participate in our own transformation.

It's the little things that count.

Allow yourself to realize the value of what you're doing by adding something new to your life and everyday routine.

Cherish the feeling of accomplishment when you get out of your comfort zone and go beyond just "thinking about it."

Pat yourself on the back!

Here's what I do to stay the course, after I've identified something I want to embrace (or tackle): Every night when I go to bed, I think about the few major things I want to accomplish the next day (or on Sundays, I look ahead to the next week).

Usually they are personal goals, business goals, tactical plans and/or family projects. I'm not a "type A" person, or so I'd like to think, but I find taking the time to organize the steps I need to take keeps my head clutter-free. It also helps me accomplish the things I want out of life and for my family.

Here are a few examples of how I work a reward system into my own life.

Baby Step:	Reward:
Spend an hour writing	Settle down with a good book to read
Wake up early to work out	Spend time with the kids over breakfast
Plan dinner in advance	Enjoy computer/TV time in the evening

"Don't wait for something big to occur. Start where you are, with what you have, and that will always lead you into something greater."

— Manin Morrissey

LOVE YOUR LIFE, AND IT WILL LOVE YOU BACK

In addition to the 10 simple steps laid out in the Reinvention Road Map, I'd like to share a few important mindset tips. When you're in the right frame of mind, you're more likely to experience success with a new endeavor.

Be kind to yourself and:

Let go of judgment. The fact that you are looking to Reinvent your life is not a sign that you did it wrong the first time around. Reinvention is an evolution. We, as humans, are constantly evolving to fulfill our higher selves. Stop judging you! Use that energy to create a better life.

Let go of guilt. Focusing on *you* is not a bad thing. In fact, your personal journey is the sole reason you are here on this planet. So let go of the guilt, and allow good to flow in its place. Feel entitled, because you are!

Be actively patient. Timing is everything and you have to trust the Universe. You don't need to change your life overnight, either. Take proactive steps to making positive changes, but also learn to practice patience as your life unfolds. Trust that perfect timing is guiding you through your transition. Practice patience with yourself and with the process of discovery.

Give yourself permission to explore. Interests and passions change over time. Don't get locked into any singular pursuit. Fling open all the doors, look under every rock. Allow your curiosity to guide you.

Never stop asking if you are happy. It is OK for dreams to change, and they can change every single day if they need to. No matter where you are in your Reinvention, make a commitment to yourself to check in and make sure that the journey you're on makes you happy.

Remember: It's never too late. I can't tell you how many people I know who have resigned themselves to being unhappy simply because they are "too old." I don't believe in age. We are as young as we feel, and if we feel we need a Reinvention, so be it!

Simply, be kind to yourself. Honor the journey, and find your own way. Let yourself dream, and liberate your wild imagination to create what you want in your life.

"Learn to value yourself, which means: fight for your own happiness."

— Ayn Rand

CONCLUSION:
GO FOR IT!
WHAT ARE YOU WAITING FOR?

"Success is a journey, not a destination.
The doing is often more important than the outcome."
— Arthur Ashe

And so, the time has come. Time to take action and bring those (little and big) dreams to life, to get on with that brilliant idea, to create that fabulous project, pursue that hobby you've been thinking about, to save a little corner of the world, to inspire yourself and others around you, for having the courage to believe in yourself enough to create a new reality.

"The journey of a thousand miles begins with one step."
— Lao Tzu

My hope is that these stories have inspired you to consider which parts of your life, your love, your self could grow from Reinvention.

Perhaps you're already reaching towards your dreams. You have a plan in place and you're making progress towards the life you know is within you.

Maybe you're quietly journaling about the things you want, but you're not quite sure how to turn them into reality.

And maybe you haven't even gotten that far.

Whatever the case — no matter what you have already learned and regardless of what mountains you face — I want to encourage you to continue to move forward on the road of Reinvention.

When it comes to Reinvention . . . trust yourself! We're all different, and we're adults with research and information on everything at our fingertips. Take in the information, and figure out what is right for you.

Reinvention really *is* possible. You just have to be prepared for bumps, challenges, sleepless nights and awe-inspiring moments of self-satisfaction. And be prepared that others will be very envious of you for having the courage to take the leap and go for what you want and definitely deserve.

You don't have to do it all in one day. In fact, you don't have to do it all *ever. Just promise yourself you will do something.*

Read a few pages of *RE:*INVENT YOUR LIFE! WHAT ARE YOU WAITING FOR? Jot down some notes and set it aside. Make a conscious effort to slow down and reflect. Call it your own personal "timeout" — time for personal nourishment, rest and reflection. It's amazing how much bigger our minds can dream when they are free to do so.

Revisit those realizations, and make a real plan to put a better life in motion. Make a true commitment to search for better and demand more. And never stop.

There should be no limit to our vision of happiness and wonderment. We should seek more every single day.

Reinvention is a journey. That's the point. If you choose to find the best and beauty in everything, you'll enjoy the journey. The choice is yours. How do you choose to live out this life?

"We were born to succeed, not to fail."
— Henry David Thoreau

After all, if there is anything we have learned through the stories I've shared here, it's that happiness — be it in our work, our relationships, our service or our own personal definition of success — truly is the ultimate goal of Reinvention. It is the only thing in the world that truly matters.

There's no right or wrong, there's no perfect plan, there's no reason you shouldn't, so just *do it*! Do it with quiet dignity, wisdom in your heart and intelligence in your body, and own the life you want with passion.

Reinventing your life comes in all shapes and sizes.

So, what are you waiting for?

ABOUT THE AUTHOR

KATHI SHARPE-ROSS

Global brand and lifestyle marketing guru Kathi Sharpe-Ross is the Founder, President and CEO of **THE SHARPE ALLIANCE** and founder of **The Reinvention Exchange**, the hub for all things "life reinvention." A sought-after marketing consultant, speaker, workshop leader, and philanthropist, she has been helping brands and businesses reinvent, build, and communicate for over 30 years. Kathi is a frequent contributor to *Huffington Post* and *Thrive Global*, and regularly interviewed on podcasts and radio.

Australian born and having grown up on three different continents, she learned at a young age how to adapt, try on new circumstances, make new friends, roll with the changes, create the tools to flourish in her world, and treat fear as an adventure. Now, in her new book, *RE:INVENT YOUR LIFE! WHAT ARE YOU WAITING FOR?* she is empowering people from all walks of life to embark on a journey toward Reinventions of "all shapes and sizes."

Kathi is married to her high school sweetheart and the mother of two fabulous grown boys. Her passions are family, friends, travel, tennis, food, art, culture and living life to its fullest.

www.TheReinventionExchange.com